ADDITIONAL ADVANCE PRAISE FOR

Marijuana Is Safer

"I have always maintained that the legalization of marijuana would lead to an overall drop in substance abuse in this country. In particular, the option of legal marijuana use, as an alternative to the death and violence associated with alcohol use, would be a welcome societal change. . . . Kudos to Fox, Armentano, and Tvert for their remarkably insightful and important book."

—GARY JOHNSON, former Republican Governor of New Mexico

"I took great pride in my performance on and off the field, and often questioned why our culture embraces alcohol while simultaneously stigmatizing those who choose to consume a less harmful alternative, marijuana. . . . This outstanding book makes it clear that it is inconsistent, both legally and socially, for our laws to punish adults who make the 'safer' choice."

—MARK STEPNOSKI, five-time NFL Pro Bowler and two-time Superbowl champion with the Dallas Cowboys

"*Marijuana Is Safer* is both informative and timely. . . . As a physician and public health educator, I highly recommend this book."

—GREGORY T. CARTER, M.D., M.S., Clinical Professor of Rehabilitation Medicine, University of Washington School of Medicine

"If you are one of the millions of Americans who support keeping marijuana illegal but enjoy a good beer, glass of wine or cocktail now and then, I suggest you read *Marijuana Is Safer*, rehab your mind, and get high on the facts. If, on the other hand, you already believe our marijuana laws are illogical, this book will give you hope that change is in the air—and show you how you can do your part to push it along."

—DAVID SIROTA, nationally syndicated columnist and bestselling author of *The Uprising* and *Hostile Takeover*

"In a society too often paralyzed by fear when it comes to finding smart solutions to our failed drug war, *Marijuana Is Safer* offers a pragmatic way forward. The authors offer a new and common sense approach to marijuana policy—one that is motivated not by incarceration or punishment, but by reducing the overall harm to our society."

—RICK STEVES, travel guidebook writer and TV and radio host

"Fox, Armentano, and Tvert offer a provocative new argument: that marijuana is actually safer to use than alcohol, so it's doubly dumb to ban the drug that's actually safer. Abstemious folks like myself may be surprised to hear that, but you'll find some solid evidence in this book."

—David Boaz, Executive Vice President of the Cato Institute, and author of *Libertarianism: A Primer* and *The Politics of Freedom*

"Readers who are new to the topic will find the pithy summaries of this complex literature easy to follow. Experts will welcome the up-to-the-minute references to the latest work on a vast range of topics. . . . Everyone will finish the text convinced that current policies need a thorough and immediate re-examination."

—Mitch Earleywine, PhD, author of *Understanding Marijuana* and editor of *Pot Politics*

"[This] is the most extensive and up-to-date book I've ever read regarding adults' relationship with the cannabis plant. . . . As challenging as its conclusion may be to the political majority, this collection of thought-provoking facts cannot be ignored."

—Rob Van Dam, former World Wrestling Entertainment (WWE) Heavyweight Champion and host of robvandam.com and RVDTV

"As the nation undergoes a shift in its thinking about drug policy, *Marijuana Is Safer* offers a timely and forceful challenge to marijuana criminalization. Anyone with an interest in drug policy, whatever their perspective, should read this important work."

—Alex Kreit, Director of the Center for Law and Social Justice, Thomas Jefferson School of Law

"In this thoroughly documented account, Fox, Armentano, and Tvert have performed a public service. They have pulled the sheet off the lie that gave us marijuana prohibition. In truth, it turns out 'The Devil Weed' is safer than alcohol. [This book] could be a game changer."

—Mike Gray, author of *Drug Crazy: How We Got Into This Mess & How We Can get Out*

"Culture and law feel, at times, impossible to change; and then suddenly we find ourselves in a whole new place. America smokes a lot of pot, America drinks a lot of booze, and pot has not always been outlawed—it stands to reason that law and culture will change again. This book seems to herald that change is now upon us.

—Jennifer Michael Hecht, PhD, author of *The Happiness Myth*

MARIJUANA IS SAFER
So Why Are We Driving People to Drink?

MARIJUANA IS SAFER
So Why Are We Driving People to Drink?

— by —

Steve Fox, Director of State Campaigns, MPP

Paul Armentano, Deputy Director, NORML

Mason Tvert, Executive Director, SAFER

Chelsea Green Publishing
White River Junction, Vermont

Project Manager: Emily Foote
Editor: Cannon Labrie
Proofreader: Helen Walden
Indexer: Peggy Holloway
Designer: Peter Holm, Sterling Hill Productions

Printed in the United States of America
First printing July, 2009
10 9 8 7 6 5 4 3 2 1 09 10 11 12 13

Our Commitment to Green Publishing
Chelsea Green sees publishing as a tool for cultural change and ecological stewardship. We
strive to align our book manufacturing practices with our editorial mission and to reduce
the impact of our business enterprise in the environment. We print our books and catalogs
on chlorine-free recycled paper, using vegetable-based inks whenever possible. This book
may cost slightly more because we use recycled paper, and we hope you'll agree that it's
worth it. Chelsea Green is a member of the Green Press Initiative (www.greenpressinitia-
tive.org), a nonprofit coalition of publishers, manufacturers, and authors working to protect the world's endangered forests and conserve natural resources. *Marijuana Is Safer* was
printed on 55-lb Rolland Enviro Natural, a 100-percent postconsumer recycled paper
supplied by Thomson-Shore.

Library of Congress Cataloging-in-Publication Data
Fox, Steve, 1964–
  Marijuana is safer : so why are we driving people to drink? / by Steve Fox, Paul
Armentano, Mason Tvert.
     p. cm.
  Includes bibliographical references and index.
  ISBN 978-1-60358-144-8
  1. Marijuana--United States. 2. Marijuana abuse--United States. 3. Alcoholism--
United States. 4. Drug legalization--United States. I. Armentano, Paul. II. Tvert, Mason.
III. Title.

  HV5822.M3F69 2009
  362.29'5--dc22

                                        200902207

Chelsea Green Publishing Company
Post Office Box 428
White River Junction, VT 05001
(802) 295-6300
www.chelseagreen.com

This book is dedicated to those
who have spoken up in support of more
rational marijuana laws, and to those who will.

Contents

Foreword

When you pick up a book touting marijuana as a safer recreational alternative to alcohol, I imagine the last thing you are expecting is a foreword from the former chief of police of a major U.S. city. Well, if you're surprised, I guess we are off to a good start. You see, the goal of this book—and the purpose of this foreword—is to encourage you (fan and foe alike) to reassess the way you think about marijuana.

In pages that follow, you will find objective comparisons of marijuana and alcohol. You will learn about the ways in which the government and other influential institutions have maintained marijuana prohibition while simultaneously turning public opinion against its use. And you will be exposed to a plethora of statistics quantifying the damage caused by alcohol use in our society. Steve, Paul, and Mason have done a terrific job of presenting all of this information in an objective, compelling, and thoughtful manner. I am certain, whatever you may think about marijuana laws at this moment, that you will look at the issue differently by the time you reach the final chapter.

But before you dive into this book—which I truly couldn't put down the first time I read it—I'd like to give you an insider's perspective on the question of marijuana versus alcohol. By "insider," I refer to my decades of law enforcement experience, during which time I witnessed firsthand how these two substances affect consumers, their families, and public safety overall. As you can imagine, those of us who have served our communities as officers of the law have encountered alcohol and marijuana users on a frequent if not daily basis, and we know all too well how often one of these two substances is associated with violent and aggressive behavior.

In all my years on the streets, it was an extremely rare occasion to have a night go by without an alcohol-related incident. More often than not, there were multiple alcohol-related calls during a shift. I became accustomed to the pattern (and the odor). If I was called to a part of town with a concentration of bars or to the local university, I could expect to be greeted by one or more drunks, flexing their "beer muscles," either in the throes of a fight or looking to start one. Sadly, the same was often true when I received a domestic abuse call. More often than not, these conflicts—many having erupted into physical violence—were fueled by one or both participants having overindulged in alcohol.

In case you might be thinking my observations are unique, let me share the results of some informal research I have conducted on my own. Over the past four years, out of a general interest in this subject, I've been asking police officers throughout the U.S. (and Canada) two questions. First: "When's the last time you had to fight someone under the influence of marijuana?" (And by this I mean marijuana only, not pot plus a six-pack or fifth of tequila.) My colleagues pause; they reflect. Their eyes widen as they realize that in their five or fifteen or thirty years on the job they have never had to fight a marijuana user. I then ask, "When's the last time you had to fight a drunk?" They look at their watches. It's telling that the booze question is answered in terms of hours, not days or weeks.

The plain and simple truth is that alcohol fuels violent behavior and marijuana does not. As described in great detail in Chapter 7, alcohol contributes to literally millions of acts of violence in the United States each year. It is a major contributing factor to crimes like domestic violence, sexual assault, and homicide. Marijuana use, on the other hand, is absent in that regard from both crime reports and the scientific literature. There is simply no causal link to be found.

As one who has been entrusted with maintaining the public's safety, I strongly believe—and most people agree—that our laws should punish people who do harm to others. This is true whether we are talking about violent crimes like murder and assault or non-violent crimes like shoplifting or insider trading. It is also appropriate to punish other behavior that threatens public safety such as speeding or driving through red lights. All of these laws are clearly designed to protect our citizens.

But by banning the use of marijuana and punishing individuals who merely possess the substance, it is difficult to see what harm we are trying to prevent. It bears repeating: From my own work and the experiences of other members of the law enforcement community, it is abundantly clear that marijuana is rarely, if ever, the cause of harmfully disruptive or violent behavior. In fact, I would go so far as to say that marijuana use often helps to tamp down tensions where they otherwise might exist.

That marijuana causes very little social harm is reason enough in a free society to legalize it for adults. But as Steve, Paul, and Mason so brilliantly demonstrate in this book, an even more persuasive reason is that by prohibiting marijuana we are steering people toward a substance that far too many people already abuse, namely alcohol. Can marijuana be abused? Of course. But, as this book makes clear, it is a much safer product for social and recreational use than alcohol. Where is the logic, then, in allowing adults to use alcohol but arresting them and branding them as criminals if they choose to use marijuana instead?

Let me be clear. The problem does not lie with law enforcement officials. Your police officers take an oath to uphold the law and cannot simply turn their backs when they see marijuana statutes violated. What we need is to replace the current system of prohibition with new laws that permit and regulate the sale of marijuana, an excellent framework for which is provided in this extraordinary book. Read it, and you'll agree it is time we stop driving the American people to drink. Instead, we should simply and logically allow them to use a safer alternative, if that is what they prefer.

NORM STAMPER
June 2009

Introduction

It's June 2004 and the city of Lisbon, Portugal, is preparing for war. Not a literal war, but an epic encounter almost as frightening in its potential for violence: England is playing France in the opening round of the Euro 2004 soccer tournament. But the showdown on the field will be nothing compared to the anticipated battle in the stands and in the streets. Soon the city will be overrun with one of Earth's most dreaded species, the English soccer fan. Branded as "hooligans," these fans are notorious for their drunken antics and their propensity to instigate alcohol-fueled fights, assaults, and, in some extreme cases, all-out riots.

So with 50,000 rabid Frenchmen and Englishmen descending upon this normally quiet town, what were the authorities to do? Ban alcohol? Not a bad guess, but no. Instead, the police announced that French and English soccer fans would not be arrested or sanctioned in any way for smoking marijuana. A spokeswoman for the Lisbon police explained the policy to Britain's *Guardian* newspaper this way: "If you are quietly smoking and a police officer is 10 meters away, what's the big risk in your behavior? I'm not going to tap you on the shoulder and ask 'What are you smoking?' if you are posing no menace to others. Our priority is alcohol."[1]

In large part because of Lisbon's novel approach, the highly anticipated match took place without incident. Police made no arrests during the game, and England's infamous hooligans behaved remarkably peacefully, even in the immediate aftermath of England's 2-1 defeat by its hated rival. Unfortunately, while this social experiment proved successful, it was short-lived. Later that evening, after English fans had drowned their sorrows at the local pubs, violence erupted among clashing fans, and several hundred people were arrested.

What's surprising about the Lisbon experience is not the outcome, which was predictable, especially since a similar lack of violence was observed when England played a soccer match in the Netherlands (where the possession of marijuana by adults is de facto legal) during the Euro 2000 tournament. Rather, it is the lack of attention the story received in the U.S. media and among policy makers. Although the Lisbon experiment was not conducted in a scientifically controlled environment, it nevertheless prompts the question: Would the legalization of marijuana reduce alcohol-related harms in society? In a country where, according to the Department of Justice, alcohol plays a pivotal role in some two-thirds of all cases of violence suffered by an intimate (such as a spouse, boyfriend, or girlfriend),[2] and is responsible for approximately 100,000 sexual assaults among young people each year,[3] this is a serious question deserving of serious discussion.

Ironically, just a few years later, the same American media that turned a collective cold shoulder to Portugal's unique experiment in "pot tolerance" became enamored with a campaign by university presidents to spur a national debate about whether to lower the drinking age in the United States to eighteen. This campaign, dubbed the Amethyst Initiative, "aims to encourage moderation and responsibility as an alternative to the drunkenness and reckless decisions about alcohol that mark the experience of many young Americans."[4] Are these university presidents also pushing for a debate about whether the legal use of marijuana could provide an alternative to "drunkenness and reckless decisions about alcohol"? Not as of this writing.

So we are left with a puzzling dichotomy. Despite knowing that a large percentage of assaults and injuries on their campuses are related to alcohol, university presidents are still willing to consider lowering the legal drinking age. Yet these same officials will not even *discuss* the idea of granting students the legal right to use a substance that is less likely to lead to violent behavior.

This is just one example of our nation's perpetual double standard surrounding the use of marijuana and alcohol. How did we as a society end up in this position? Why do we criminally arrest or discipline people for consuming a substance that is not associated with acts of violence, yet tolerate and at times even celebrate the use of another that is? Why do we embrace the use of alcohol, a toxic substance whose consumption is responsible for hundreds of acute alcohol-poisoning deaths in the United States each year, while at the same time condemn the use of marijuana, which is incapable of causing a fatal overdose? Although marijuana remains the third most frequently consumed drug of choice in America, trailing in popularity only behind alcohol and tobacco, these questions have never been addressed at length by either the media or America's elected officials. This is about to change.

Americans have a unique, if slightly schizophrenic, relationship with Mary Jane. On one hand, the U.S. government reports that over 100 million U.S. citizens—that's nearly 43 percent of the population over twelve years of age—admit that they've smoked pot.[5] On the other hand, marijuana possession and recreational use is illegal in all fifty states. (We should note, for factual accuracy, that the private use of marijuana inside the home is legal in Alaska, based on a state court determination that it is protected under a right to privacy. In addition, as of this writing, the medical use of cannabis is legal in thirteen states.) Cannabis has been described—by an administrative law judge at the U.S. Drug Enforcement Administration, no less—as "one of the safest therapeutically active substances known to man."[6] Yet the federal government stubbornly classifies it under federal law as one of society's most dangerous· drugs. Hollywood actors unabashedly simulate pot smoking in movies and on television, much to audiences' delight. Meanwhile, this same behavior is criticized and discouraged in government-sponsored public service announcements on the very same screens.

One might wonder how a substance so universally demonized by America's elected officials remains so popular among the American public. Perhaps the answer is that politicians and the mainstream media are just reinforcing each others' talking points, while much of the rest of America now accepts marijuana for what it is—a relatively benign substance that is frequently used responsibly by millions of people. Well, that may be the case for a certain segment of the population, but this enlightened attitude is far from universal.

Despite pot's popularity, surveys indicate that many people—nonusers in particular—tend to overestimate the drug's actual harms. Not necessarily to the same degree as the federal government, mind you, but nonetheless much of the public still holds many misconceptions about the plant and its effects. In fact, some one-fifth to one-third of Americans assume that pot is *more harmful* than booze. Another one-third of Americans consider marijuana to be equally as harmful as alcohol.

It is our contention that these misconceptions about pot's alleged dangers are the primary obstacle to changing marijuana laws in this country. Therefore, our goal is to demonstrate to you, the reader, that marijuana is not only less harmful than alcohol, but that the difference is really quite significant.

This is not to say that cannabis is harmless. No rational person would make this assertion, and indeed we have dedicated a portion of this book to addressing pot's potential health hazards. Nevertheless, almost all drugs, including many that are legal, pose greater threats to individual health than does marijuana. To date, virtually every federally commissioned government study ever conducted on the subject affirms this conclusion.

But don't expect your government to highlight this fact or even stay neutral on the issue. Rather, most politicians and law enforcement officials today rely on gross distortions and exaggerations

regarding pot's supposed dangers—call it "Reefer Madness redux"—
to justify their failed and destructive prohibitionist policies. In this
book, we provide ample scientific evidence contradicting a number
of the government's more popular and egregious marijuana myths.
Readers will learn the facts surrounding the alleged "new dangers"
of today's supposedly superpotent pot. We will also examine just
how harmful marijuana smoke is to the lungs, and what association,
if any, there is between the use of cannabis and harder drugs. The
answers may surprise you.

One might ask, if marijuana poses so few legitimate harms to
health and society—in fact, far fewer than those posed by alcohol—
then why does the federal government spend tens of millions of dollars annually on Web sites and public advertising campaigns primarily
designed to maintain the criminal prohibition of cannabis? Is the
feds' fixation on pot a moral crusade or part of a larger cultural battle?
Regardless of the government's underlying motivation, it is beyond
dispute that politicians and members of law enforcement have sys-
tematically demonized pot to such a degree that a significant portion
of Americans still support criminalizing the recreational use of marijuana—even though it could lead to the arresting and jailing of their
friends, neighbors, and perhaps, even family members.

Of course, the dissemination of antimarijuana propaganda is not
our government's sole means of marijuana demonization. Where
persuasion does not suffice, there is always the threat of punishment. The federal government, as well as every state in the nation
(except Alaska), prohibits the possession and cultivation of marijuana for recreational use, with state penalties ranging from $100
fines (in Ohio) to life in prison (in Oklahoma). Since 1965, police
have arrested an estimated twenty million Americans for marijuana-
related crimes—mostly for simple possession. This figure is roughly
equal to the combined populations of Colorado, Massachusetts, and
New Jersey. While a relatively small portion of first-time offenders
arrested for marijuana possession are sentenced to time in jail, the
fact remains that the repercussions of the arrest alone are significant.

The potential sanctions include:

- loss of driving privileges;
- loss of federal college aid;
- loss of personal private property;
- revocation of professional driver's license;
- loss of certain welfare benefits such as food stamps;
- removal from public housing; and
- loss of child custody.

Cannabis consumers are also subject to additional punishments stemming from the now nearly ubiquitous specter of drug testing. Depending on the circumstances, individuals who test positive for having consumed pot at some previous, unspecified point in time may lose their jobs, be suspended from school or barred from participating in extracurricular activities, be forced to enter a "drug treatment" program, have their parole revoked, or even be stripped of an Olympic medal.

We contend that the ultimate, if unintended, impact of the government's extreme antimarijuana laws and propaganda is to push people away from cannabis and toward consuming alcohol. If students learn that they may lose their financial aid if they use cannabis, but will most likely receive a slap on the wrist—at worst—for drinking alcohol while underage, which option are they likely to choose? A similar incentive is created in many workplaces that impose random drug testing. Employees know that they can spend their off-hours drunk as skunks with nothing more to fear than some lost productivity if they arrive to work hungover the next morning. Yet if an employee at the same company is randomly drug tested on Monday after relaxing with friends and enjoying a joint the preceding Friday, he or she may be searching for a new job within the week.

The irony is that these policies implicitly motivate people to use what is an objectively more harmful substance. Studies by the National Academy of Sciences and others have demonstrated that alcohol is significantly more addictive than marijuana. Moreover, chronic alcohol use, as well as acute intoxication, can lead to organ damage and death. According to the National Institute on Alcohol Abuse and Alcoholism, more than 35,000 Americans die annually as the direct result of alcohol consumption.[7] By contrast, no study to date has ever identified a link between long-term marijuana use and increased mortality—meaning, researchers have not identified *any* way in which long-term marijuana use hastens death.

Alcohol has also been shown, in contrast to marijuana, to fuel aggressive, violent behavior. In one study of domestic violence, researchers found that men were eight times more likely to be abusive on days when they consumed alcohol as compared to days when they did not.[8] Overall, the U.S. government estimates that alcohol contributes to 25 to 30 percent of *all* violent crime in America.[9] In the United Kingdom, the association between alcohol and violence may be even more pronounced. In 2004, the *Guardian* newspaper reported that the police minister planned to "blitz alcohol violence [that coming] summer, in the face of Home Office research showing that alcohol is the root cause of nearly half of all violent crime, and of 70% of hospital emergency and accident admissions at peak times."[10]

So what can we do to ensure that individuals have the freedom to choose marijuana instead of alcohol without risking arrest, jail, and their very livelihoods? The obvious answer is that we need to amend federal and state laws that criminalize the possession and use of marijuana by adults. But how does one go about doing so?

On this topic we speak from experience, having worked for more than twenty-three years combined at three of the nation's most prominent organizations dedicated to reforming marijuana laws— the Marijuana Policy Project (MPP), the National Organization for the Reform of Marijuana Laws (NORML), and Safer Alternative for Enjoyable Recreation (SAFER). Through public-education campaigns, state and federal lobbying efforts, and state and local ballot initiative campaigns, these three groups have helped to diminish anti-marijuana sentiment in America. However, prior to the establishment of SAFER in 2005, no organization had single-mindedly engaged in the strategy outlined in this text: that is, a high-profile, public-education campaign focused entirely on the fact that marijuana is objectively safer than alcohol, both for the user and for society.

Past efforts to reform marijuana laws in this country have typically made only passing references to the marijuana-versus-alcohol comparison. Instead, they have emphasized other, more conventional arguments, many of which we will discuss in greater detail later in this book. One such contention is that it is a waste of law enforcement resources to arrest and prosecute marijuana users. Although arguments like this are valid, they have so far failed to convince our elected officials—or even a majority of the American public—to legalize, tax, and regulate marijuana. Instead, reformers are all too often confronted by citizens and elected officials echoing one common refrain: "Why should society legalize another vice?" In essence, much of the public and its elected officials, having witnessed firsthand the many problems associated with alcohol, are hesitant to give a green light to another intoxicant—regardless of what its relative harms may be.

In the face of this obstacle, many advocates have downplayed discussing the relative harms of the two substances. Instead they have simply argued that marijuana should be "treated like alcohol"—in other words, it should be sold legally and regulated. Although we agree with this conclusion, the call to treat marijuana like alcohol does little to alter the underlying public perception that marijuana is "bad" or "dangerous" and, therefore, is no more than another unnecessary vice. Until we force the public to appreciate that the legalization of marijuana would not be "adding a vice," but instead would be providing adults with a less harmful recreational alternative, legalization will likely remain—pardon the pun—a pipe dream.

Of course, educating the public about the relative harms of cannabis and alcohol will not be accomplished through a top-down, government-run advertising campaign. It will require a broad movement of citizens willing to speak honestly and openly about the relative harms and benefits of the two substances. We hope this book, which is designed to both educate and inspire, will become an essential part of that movement. Whether you are a cannabis connoisseur seeking to educate friends and family or someone who has never even seen a marijuana plant outside of a television or movie screen, we are certain that you will benefit from reading the pages that follow.

This book is divided into three parts. In part 1 we compare and contrast the social and public health impact of cannabis and alcohol. We examine the popularity of each drug, as well as the potential harms each one presents to the user and to society. Part 2 details the various ways our government has attempted to outlaw and demonize marijuana over the past seventy-plus years, and explains how these policies are driving people to drink. In part 3 we provide an overview of past attempts to reform America's marijuana laws and propose an alternative, citizen-driven public-education campaign based on the message that marijuana is safer than alcohol. Finally, we offer our vision for a future in which cannabis is regulated and controlled like alcohol, with laws limiting pot's sales to licensed establishments and mandating the enforcement of proper age controls.

In the latter part of the book, we have also included tips and resources for those of you who want to spread the "marijuana is safer than alcohol" message among your friends, on your campus, or in your communities. If this book touches you, we hope you will join us in our mission to educate the public and help us bring about an end to marijuana prohibition.

STEVE FOX
Director of State Campaigns, MPP

PAUL ARMENTANO
Deputy Director, NORML

MASON TVERT
Executive Director, SAFER

PART ONE

The Choice: Marijuana vs. Alcohol

chapter one

The Big Two: The Popular Acceptance and Use of Marijuana and Alcohol

In America, two competing parties dominate the political landscape: Democrats and Republicans. In the battle for fast-food supremacy, the two leading combatants are McDonald's and Burger King. When it comes to soft drinks, two rival brands stand out above all others: Coke and Pepsi. And when it comes to recreational intoxicants, the choice is clear: there's alcohol, and there's marijuana.

Alcohol and Marijuana Use Through the Ages

If you're like most people reading this book, there's a fairly good chance that you've been "high" from either pot or booze at some point in your life. Don't worry, we won't tell anyone. And, quite frankly, for those of you who have been high, there's nothing to be particularly ashamed or embarrassed about.

Many experts believe that humans possess an intrinsic drive to deliberately alter their consciousness through the use of intoxicating substances. University of California at Los Angeles professor Ronald Siegel argues that this desire is biological, on par with such survival instincts as thirst and hunger.[1] He's hardly alone in his assessment.

Writing in the 2003 book *Out of It: A Cultural History of Intoxication*, British journalist Stuart Walton similarly determined: "Intoxication is a universal human theme. There are no recorded instances of fully formed societies anywhere in history that have lived without the use of psychoactive substances."[2] One of the world's leading scholars on the subject, best-selling author and noted physician Dr. Andrew Weil, agrees. "Drug use is universal," he concludes. "Every human culture in every age of history has used one or more psychoactive drugs. . . . In fact, drug-taking is so common that it seems to be a basic human activity."[3]

According to some researchers, humans started manufacturing beer almost as soon as they began harvesting barley (about 8000 B.C.E.). In the book *Alcoholism: The Facts* Ann Manzardo states that fermented fruit juices (wine) and grains (beer) were human beings' "earliest beverage of choice." She jokes, "A long-standing debate in archeology centers on the question of which came first after the domestication of barley—beer or bread?"[4]

The cultivation of marijuana can similarly be traced back many thousands of years. Cannabis-based textiles dating to 7000 B.C.E. have been recovered in northern China, and the plant's use as a psychoactive agent goes back nearly as far. Archeologists in Central Asia recently discovered over two pounds of cannabis in the 2,700-year-old grave of an ancient shaman. After scientists conducted extensive testing of the material's potency, they concluded that the ancients were using cannabis for medicinal and euphoric purposes: "No obvious male cannabis plant parts . . . were evident, implying their exclusion or possible removal by human intervention, as these are pharmacologically less psychoactive," investigators concluded. "The results presented collectively point to the most probable conclusion which is that [ancient] culture[s] cultivated cannabis for pharmaceutical, psychoactive or divinatory purposes."[5]

The Use of Alcohol and Marijuana Today

Today, hundreds of millions of people worldwide have used alcohol and cannabis at some point during their lifetime. A 2008 World Health Organization (WHO) examination of the licit and illicit drug habits of adults in seventeen separate countries provides the intoxicating details.[6]

According to the study, more than 90 percent of Americans have consumed alcohol during their lives, and almost 45 percent have used marijuana. Second only to the United States in pot consumption is New Zealand, where some 42 percent of the population has smoked weed, and a whopping 95 percent has drunk booze. Among the European nations included in the study, Ukraine reported the highest percentage of alcohol users (97 percent of the population), as well as the lowest percentage of pot smokers (6.5 percent). In the Netherlands, where weed may be ingested legally, 93 percent of the population has consumed alcohol and 20 percent has tried cannabis. These percentages were nearly identical in neighboring France and Germany, even though both countries impose strict criminal restrictions on pot use.

In Israel, only 58 percent of the population has consumed alcohol, and nearly 12 percent of the public admits having tried pot. In Mexico, 86 percent of respondents said that they had consumed booze, while 8 percent said they'd used marijuana. Finally, in South Africa, only 40 percent of the public admitted that they had drunk alcohol, but nearly 10 percent said that they had smoked pot. Ironically, the WHO study found that the United States possesses the planet's highest rate of lifetime marijuana consumption despite imposing some of the world's harshest antipot penalties.

So just how many Americans *regularly* consume pot and alcohol? Let's look at booze first. According to 2007 data published by the U.S. Department of Health and Human Services, approximately 66 percent of the population aged twelve or older (roughly 163 million Americans) imbibed alcohol during the past year, and just over half of all Americans (127 million) drink booze regularly.[7] Of these, nearly one-quarter of Americans (58 million) engage in binge drinking (consuming an unhealthy quantity of alcohol in one sitting), and 7 percent (slightly more than 10 percent of those who drink) meet the criteria for problem or "at risk" drinkers. Notably, despite the prohibition on the sale and recreational use of alcohol for those under age twenty-one, the U.S. government reports that in 2007, more than three out of four twenty-year-olds had consumed alcohol in the past year, and nearly 60 percent had done so in the past month.[8]

In comparison, how many Americans regularly smoke pot? Because the use of marijuana is illegal it's impossible to know for sure. Fortunately, we do have some estimates. Every year, researchers from the United States Substance Abuse Mental Health Services Administration (SAMHSA) poll Americans regarding their use of licit and illicit substances. According to SAMHSA's admittedly conservative figures—respondents tend to underestimate their use of *legal* intoxicants by as much as 30 percent on government polls, and most experts assume that Americans' illegal drug use is even more grossly underreported—roughly 25 million Americans (10 percent of the population aged twelve or older) have consumed cannabis in the past year, and 15 million (6 percent) define themselves as regular (at least once per month) users.[9] Like alcohol, marijuana use also remains popular, if illegal, among youth. According to annual survey data compiled by the University of Michigan at Ann Arbor, between 40 and 50 percent of graduating high school seniors acknowledge having tried pot, a figure that has changed little since the mid-1970s.[10]

From an economic perspective, both drug markets are now multibillion-dollar industries. According to a 2006 Columbia University report, Americans spend over $130 billion annually on alcohol.[11] Predictably, the commercial marketing of booze is also big business. According to a 2008 Georgetown University study, the alcohol industry bought over 340,000 television ads in 2007 (up more than 50 percent from 2001), totaling just under $1 billion. Since 2001,

Anheuser-Busch Company has spent over $2.2 billion placing television ads, followed by Miller and Molson/Coors.[12]

By contrast, no commercial advertising dollars are spent marketing marijuana to the public—aside from the tens of millions of dollars spent annually by the federal government to *discourage* pot use. Nevertheless, experts estimate the retail value of the domestic marijuana market to be $113 billion per year[13]—a figure that rivals alcohol. Today, marijuana is the largest retail cash crop in the United States, far outpacing the value of corn, soybeans, and hay.[14] Moreover, government figures indicate that U.S. marijuana cultivation is a rapidly growing industry. According to a 2005 State Department report, domestic cannabis cultivation in the United States totals some 10,000 metric tons per year (more than 22 million pounds).[15] This total is *ten times* the amount produced in the early 1980s.

"Drink Life": The Portrayal of Booze in Popular Culture

Although booze and pot are woven into the fabric of America's popular culture, they are typically portrayed in entirely different ways. The use of alcohol by adults is marketed aggressively, celebrated openly, and is normally depicted by the media in a positive manner. That's why most Americans give little, if any, thought to the moral and health implications surrounding the use of alcohol, and many could not imagine a society that was anything but accepting of the public's "right" to drink.

Just for a moment we'd like you think about your own social routine. Now think about how often alcohol plays a role in your activities. For instance, have you ever given wine to a family member as a gift during the holidays? Chances are, you have. Ever gotten together with friends to have some beers and watch a sporting event on television? Or asked your colleagues to "grab a drink" after work? Of course you have. Who hasn't? And what about the last time you attended a wedding ceremony? Friends and families "celebrated" the marriage by toasting the bride and groom with a glass of champagne, didn't they? Sure they did; after all, it's the customary thing to do.

In virtually all of these examples, people don't really think about how or why they're consuming alcohol. Rather, the use of booze is simply viewed as a traditionally and socially acceptable means to complement a festive occasion—no more, no less.

Now think about how often you are exposed to images glamorizing the use of alcohol. Even if you don't drink booze, all one has to do is turn on the television—a billion dollars in TV advertising goes a long way—to witness the various ways in which contemporary culture glorifies the consumption of alcohol. For example, a national marketing campaign for one top-selling American beer commands consumers to "drink life," as if to imply that those who imbibe get more satisfaction and enjoyment out of their days and nights than those who abstain from booze. A prominent series of ads for another top-selling brand implies that nothing else but a cold beer can sufficiently counter the aftereffects of a long, hard workday. In fact the very term "happy hour" (or its brand-specific equivalent, "It's Miller time!") is synonymous with the use of alcohol at the end of the day. Conveniently, this ubiquitous phrase promotes the positive, euphoric effects of alcohol while making no mention of the drug's downsides—such as the hangover that might follow the next day.

During the 1980s and early 1990s, one of television's most popular sitcoms was the lighthearted barroom drama *Cheers*, where a cast of lovable characters routinely bantered over beers at a local watering hole "where everybody knows your name." Alcohol-fueled arguments, fistfights, and regrettable drunken hookups—frequent occurrences at most bars on any given Friday or Saturday night—were rarely incorporated into the show's plot during its eleven-year run. And, aside from some friendly ribbing, there were few complaints that the characters' consumption of alcohol made them hopelessly unproductive—although they routinely spent a significant part of their day sitting at a bar.

How many of you reading this book routinely watch professional sports on television? How often have you witnessed pro athletes celebrate important wins by publicly dousing one another—and usually, in recent years, at least one attractive female broadcaster—with beer and champagne? Curiously, were a group of nonathletes to engage in similar behavior at, let's say, a private fraternity party, there's no doubt that their actions would be castigated (and rightly so) as alcohol abuse and sexual harassment. Yet this same behavior is routinely aired on primetime network television following major sporting events without any thought given to the "message" these activities might be sending to younger viewers.

Sports stars also frequently serve as pitchmen for alcohol products. After all, what child of the 1970s can forget watching their football and baseball heroes comically debating whether Miller Lite beer "tastes great" or was "less filling"? (The memorable ad campaign, which Miller launched in 1976, was selected as one of the top ten best ad campaigns of the twentieth century by *Advertising Age* magazine.[16])

The alcohol industry is a prominent sponsor of professional sporting events—Major League Baseball's Colorado Rockies play in Coors Field, for instance—as well as a prominent advertiser during televised games. Booze is also a staple of "tailgating"—a longstanding and much revered tradition where sports fans camp out in the stadium parking lot prior to a game and drink copious amounts of alcohol. Notably, this tradition is exceedingly popular among college-age sports fans, many of whom are under the legal age for alcohol consumption.

This Bud's For You: The Portrayal of Pot in Popular Culture

While cultural references to cannabis may not be as common as those pertaining to booze, they are becoming more prevalent and prominent—even if the plant's illicit status discourages many of its consumers from identifying themselves publicly. For instance, references and accolades about the use of pot are widespread in popular music. Numerous top-selling hip-hop artists like Snoop Dogg, Dr. Dre, Cypress Hill, and Redman brazenly celebrate weed in their lyrics. Similarly, rapper Method Man titled his 2006 album "4:21 . . . The Day After" in an effort to appeal to marijuana-friendly audiences. (April 20 is a date that is widely recognized in cannabis culture as a day to celebrate the use of marijuana.)

Country music heavyweight Willie Nelson's fondness for marijuana is similarly well known. In 2005, the artist adorned the cover of his CD *Countryman* with a marijuana leaf. Nelson also serves as a spokesperson for the National Organization for the Reform of Marijuana Laws (NORML). Reggae legends Bob Marley ("Ganja Gun") and Peter Tosh ("Legalize It") were similarly outspoken about their pot use. Today, even heavy metal fans have a "pot-friendly" musical subgenre known as "stoner rock,"—so-named because of the bands', as well as their fans', affinity for weed.

Affectionate references to cannabis are equally popular in film and on television. Late-night hosts like Jon Stewart, Bill Maher, and Jay Leno liberally sprinkle their monologues with jokes about weed. While many of their punch lines seize upon various marijuana stereotypes, the hosts are just as likely to elicit laughs from the audience by poking fun of politicians' all-too-often antiquated attitudes toward the plant. (We provide readers with a profile of one prominent politician's pot gaffe in chapter 2.)

Hollywood is also cashing in on Americans' fondness for marijuana—a trend described in 2008 by the *Christian Science Monitor* as cinema's new "stoned age."[17] Successful films and cable television shows like *Weeds, Harold and Kumar Go to White Castle, Half-Baked, Pineapple Express, Entourage, Dazed and Confused,* and *How High?* not only utilize marijuana-themed plots and characters, but also incorporate cannabis into their marketing. For example, distributors for *Harold and Kumar Escape from Guantanamo Bay* and *Reefer Madness: The Movie Musical* both chose to debut their films around

April 20. Writing in 2008 about Hollywood's growing acceptance of pot, Canadian reporters Ben Carrozza and Leah Collins concluded, "With pot-friendly flicks often scoring huge at the box office—and earning bags of pop culture credibility—stoners are almost mainstream."[18]

Many prominent actors and directors are outspoken about their past or current use of cannabis. Award-winning filmmakers Robert Altman (*MASH, Nashville*) and Oliver Stone (*JFK, Born on the Fourth of July*) both have admitted to being lifelong cannabis consumers. Shortly before his death in 2006 at age eighty-one, Altman told a British newspaper, "At the end of the day you want to have a laugh and sit down and smoke a joint, which I do every day of my life."[19] Meanwhile in front of the camera, "A-list" celebrities like Jennifer Aniston, Sarah Silverman, Brad Pitt, Seth Rogan, Matthew McConaughey, and Woody Harrelson are some of the Screen Actors Guild's most successful pot smokers. Harrelson's support for the rights of cannabis consumers is so strong that he once withheld several thousand dollars in federal taxes to protest the government's prohibition of marijuana. He is also an active member of the advisory board for NORML.

Certainly all of you reading this book are aware that many prominent American politicians have dabbled with herb. And while twenty years ago the political fallout of such an admission was quick and severe—in the mid-1980s, Supreme Court nominee Douglas Ginsberg was withdrawn from consideration for having admitted using pot in college—well, the times they are a changin'. In the 1990s, two-term Democratic president Bill Clinton famously acknowledged trying pot (although he alleged that he "didn't inhale"), while his arch nemesis, former Republican House Speaker Newt Gingrich, dismissed his own past marijuana use as "a sign we were alive." By the 2004 presidential election, the use of marijuana by presidential candidates had become so passé that candidate Joseph Lieberman publicly apologized during a nationally televised debate for *not* having tried the drug. During his 2008 presidential campaign,

Barack Obama also spoke openly about his own pot use, admitting, "I inhaled frequently; that was the point." The live audience—many of whom had also undoubtedly "inhaled frequently" from time to time—applauded Obama's candid remark. The statement galvanized Obama's support among young people, many of whom either had used or continue to use pot, and all but secured votes from America's budding cannabis community.

Of course given the herb's criminal status and the numerous penalties associated with its use, the fact that there exists *any* pot culture—much less one that is as prominent as cannabis culture—is a testament to how many people consume marijuana and view the plant favorably. Opining in the July 7, 2008 edition of the *Central Florida Future* newspaper, a student columnist aptly wrote, "Marijuana is one of the only illegal substances so influential in American culture that its users have developed a sub-culture of their own." The author continued: "Weed culture is a nationwide phenomenon complete with films, music, books, stores and silly T-shirts; all dedicated to America's favorite criminal pastime. It's a culture with its own heroes, like Bob Marley, Willie Nelson, Cheech and Chong. A pot leaf is more than just a picture of a drug; it is a symbol that connects people to a lifestyle."[20]

The Marijuana Constituency

At the turn of the twentieth century, tens of thousands of concerned citizens joined together to lobby for the prohibition of alcohol. They succeeded. In 1919, the Eighteenth Amendment to the U.S. Constitution was ratified, prohibiting the public sale and consumption of booze. Thirteen years later, tens of thousands of concerned citizens joined together again to lobby for the repeal of alcohol prohibition. They also succeeded. Today, tens of thousands, if not hundreds of thousands, of concerned citizens are once again lobbying their government for a repeal of prohibition—pot prohibition.

Unlike other illegal substances, marijuana has its own self-identified, vocal, grassroots constituency. Today, a variety of social advocacy groups such as NORML, the Marijuana Policy Project (MPP), and SAFER work full-time on their behalf. In fact, NORML proudly bills itself as the "marijuana smokers lobby." Combined, these and other like-minded organizations have tens of thousands of members and annual budgets of several millions of dollars.

Of course these budgets, as impressive as they are, pale in comparison to the financial resources available to groups that lobby on behalf of the alcohol manufacturers. Organizations like the Beer Institute, the Wine Institute, the Distilled Spirits Council of the United States, and the National Beer Wholesalers Association (NBWA) employ large staffs and make substantial financial contributions to politicians of both parties. These groups also engage in grassroots organizing. For example, the NBWA has members in every congressional district across the country, and Anheuser-Busch employs a company lobbyist in every state capital.[21]

Despite possessing significantly fewer financial resources, groups like NORML, MPP, and SAFER, as well as their supporters, also play an active role in local and state politics. In recent years all three groups have sponsored successful campaigns to liberalize marijuana penalties at the local and state level. These organizations and their constituents are also becoming more and more engaged in federal politics. Notably, marijuana-law reformers in December 2008 made their voices heard on the Web site Change.gov, the official site of the Obama administration transition team, during an online poll to determine the nation's top public policy priorities. Of the 7,300 different questions voted on by the public, more than a dozen of the top 50 pertained to fixing America's pot laws, and the number 1 question was: "Will [the U.S. government] consider legalizing marijuana so that [it] can regulate it, tax it, put age limits on it, and create millions of new jobs and create a billion dollar industry right here in the U.S.?"[22]

So there you have it. On the surface, marijuana and alcohol are simply two popular substances—nothing more, nothing less. But obviously there is something more. One substance is legal and the other is not. But before we tackle that reality starting in chapter 4, let's spend a couple of chapters examining these two drugs in greater detail.

chapter two

Pot 101:
Understanding Marijuana

For more than three decades, Democratic congressman Tom Harkin has served as a reasoned voice for the health and welfare of America's rural communities. While in Washington, he has spearheaded federal efforts to expand funding for medical research and alternative energy programs. Among his peers and his constituents, Harkin is well known for his commitment to civil liberties—having successfully championed the Americans with Disabilities Act, which prohibits discrimination against those with mental and physical disabilities.

By almost all appearances, Senator Harkin is a compassionate, well-educated, rational human being—just the sort of person that most Americans want representing them in Congress. However, bring up the topic of marijuana and a seldom seen side of Harkin's personality rises to the surface—one that shares more in common with the "Reefer Madness" era of the 1930s than reflects the situation today.

In 2008, an Iowa NORML member wrote to Harkin and asked him to explain why he supports the criminal prohibition of marijuana. The lawmaker's reply: "[M]arijuana is not the recreational drug that many people believe it to be. [M]arijuana use often has fatal consequences."

Within days, the senator's over-the-top response was eliciting tongue-and-cheek media snippets nationwide. On the Internet, tens of thousands of Americans logged onto the Web site of Washington, D.C., gossip columnist Wonkette (Ana Marie Cox), who mockingly posted the headline: "Senator Tom Harkin: Marijuana Makes People Sell Their Children."[1] In the eyes of many, particularly those tens of millions of adults who use or had ever used marijuana, the remarks turned the onetime U.S. presidential candidate into an immediate laughingstock—the poster child for what some Americans *don't* know about pot. Unfortunately, such marijuana ignorance is hardly limited to one lone senator from Iowa.

———

Although marijuana is the most widely used illicit intoxicant in the United States (and the world), much of the public—and apparently some prominent politicians—still remain woefully ignorant about the plant's multiple uses and its psychoactive effects. There are several reasons for this confusion.

For starters, independent public opinion polls indicate that only about one-half of the American population admits to having had firsthand experience with cannabis.[2] Further, among those who have tried pot, some only experimented with the drug on a handful of occasions. Many others ceased their use altogether decades ago.

Additionally, society is bombarded with varying, and often contradictory, messages about pot. The White House Office of National Drug Control Policy (more commonly known as the drug czar's office) has spent tens of millions of taxpayers' dollars per year to produce print and television advertisements stigmatizing marijuana—blaming its use for a host of societal ills. Conversely, national advocacy groups like NORML, SAFER, and the Marijuana Policy Project engage in national outreach and media campaigns rebutting many of the U.S. government's widespread and oft-repeated claims—most of which are based on rhetoric and stereotypes rather than scientific facts.

Law enforcement organizations also muddy the waters, often distorting the facts about marijuana to the mainstream media and to young people (via so-called drug-education programs like Drug Abuse Resistance Education, or DARE,[3] which is taught in some three out of four U.S. public schools). Indeed, these days it's hardly hyperbole for young people to say, "Everything I ever learned about marijuana I learned in junior high—and all of it was wrong."

We're here to inform you and to set the record straight. To be clear, the information that follows is not just for people who have never been exposed to marijuana. Even most occasional users of cannabis have only a surface knowledge of the drug and are in need of a crash course in Marijuana 101.

To give you a sense of what we mean, think for a moment about your knowledge of alcohol. Although you may assume that you don't know much about booze, and that moreover, there isn't much to know—people drink, they get drunk, and that's that—it's quite likely that you know far more than you think you do. You certainly know that there are many kinds of alcohol legally available for consumption—such as beer, wine, schnapps, vodka, rum, whiskey, and even pure grain alcohol. You are aware that these beverages vary greatly in terms of their intoxicating effects. For example, there is a huge difference between 12 ounces of beer and 12 ounces of vodka. You probably even know a thing or two about the alcohol content of various beverages, that beer is about 3 percent alcohol by volume, and hard liquor is described in terms of proof, which actually represents twice the percentage of alcohol in the beverage (e.g., 80 proof vodka is 40 percent alcohol by volume). You also likely know that different types of alcohol produce different effects. For instance, red wine has a tendency to make people feel sleepy and trigger migraine headaches, while white wine does not.

By contrast, what do you *know* about pot?

If you are like the vast majority of Americans, when you think about pot your thoughts pretty much start and stop with the word marijuana itself. In other words, you probably perceive "marijuana" as a generic term like "aspirin." But that is certainly not the case. Today, there are nearly as many varieties of marijuana as there are alcohol, each with different names, potencies, purposes, and effects.

In the pages that follow, we aim to close the gap between your knowledge about alcohol and your knowledge about pot. Our aim is to provide you with a basic understanding of the marijuana plant, including its active components and its effects on those who use it. By doing so, we hope to address many readers' stereotypes and preconceptions regarding the cannabis plant so that they can better make an assessment of whether adults should have legal access to it.

What Is Marijuana?

When we step back and think about it, it's hard to believe that we really need to have this discussion at all. As we noted in chapter 1, humans have been using marijuana as an intoxicant for thousands of years, and according to a 2008 medical journal review, there are now more than 17,000 published studies and papers available in the scientific literature analyzing pot, its constituents, and their effects on the human body.[4] In short, marijuana is one of the most studied and widely used plants in human existence. Yet despite marijuana's exceedingly long and detailed history, many people today are unfamiliar with the plant's effects and pharmacology. Here are some basics.

The term *marijuana* is Mexican in origin and is typically used to refer to any part of—or any one of—the three distinctive species of the cannabis plant: *Cannabis sativa* (which tends to grow tall and stalky), *Cannabis indica* (which tends to grow smaller and bushier), or *Cannabis ruderalis* (a wild-growing species of cannabis found primarily in Russia and Eastern Europe). Grown outdoors, the cannabis plant will typically reach maturity within three to five months. Grown indoors, under optimum heat and lighting, the plant may reach maturity within as few as sixty days.

Humans have used various parts of the cannabis plant for a multitude of purposes. Most people are aware that marijuana is used as an intoxicant, but far fewer know that certain varieties of cannabis—as well as most parts of the plant, including the seeds and the stalk—contain virtually no psychoactive properties yet offer many other potential benefits. For example, ground seeds from the marijuana plant contain uniquely high and balanced levels of essential amino acids and essential fatty acids and may be baked into a variety of nutritional foodstuffs, such as bread, butter, and salad dressing. Oil can also be processed from cannabis seeds and used for sautéing or consumed as a nutritional supplement. Since the seeds contain no euphoria-producing compounds, the importation and domestic sale of certain cannabis-based foods, oils, and sterilized seeds is permitted in the United States.

The stalk of the marijuana plant, primarily of the *Cannabis sativa* variety—which can grow to twenty feet in height—can also be harvested for its bast fiber content. Most industrialized nations, including Canada, Japan, Australia, and the European Union, regulate the commercial production of low-potency varieties of cannabis, commonly called hemp, for industrial purposes.[5] This practice is hardly new. During America's colonial era, many of the founding fathers, including George Washington and Thomas Jefferson, espoused cultivating cannabis for the production of rope, sails, cloth, and paper.[6] In fact, as recently as during World War II the U.S. government commissioned tens of thousands of domestic farmers to grow marijuana to assist with America's wartime needs. (A 1943 film produced by the U.S. Department of Agriculture, entitled *Hemp For Victory*, calls the plant "indispensable . . . in the service of mankind.") Following the War's conclusion, however, the U.S. government imposed a complete ban on the domestic production of the plant, including the cultivation of non-psychoactive *Cannabis sativa* varieties. Nevertheless, tens of millions of wild plants, remnants from these once government-subsidized plots, continue to grow throughout the United States, primarily in the Midwest. As mandated by federal law—which makes no distinction among cannabis species—police destroy some two hundred million of these plants annually. As a result, U.S. retailers who produce hemp-based clothing and other products must exclusively import cannabis fiber from overseas.

Active but not necessarily psychoactive components of the cannabis plant, known as cannabinoids, possess a variety of therapeutic applications. Although we will explore this issue in greater depth in chapter 3, we would be remiss if we did not at least mention marijuana's historic and current applications as a medicinal herb here.

At the time this book went to print, thirteen states allowed for the legal, physician-supervised use of medical marijuana by state-qualified patients. The plant's therapeutic constituents are typically used by patients for their analgesic (pain-reducing), anxiolytic (stress-reducing), and mood-elevating properties. Compounds in marijuana are also effective at reducing nausea and stimulating appetite. Today doctors can prescribe an FDA-approved medication to treat these symptoms called Marinol. Available in pill form only, Marinol is actually a synthetic version of THC, the primary psychoactive chemical in the marijuana plant. Numerous other therapeutic applications for cannabis have also been documented in recent years, including neuroprotective, antibacterial, and even cancer-fighting properties.

Of course, most people associate marijuana with its euphoria-inducing qualities. Throughout history human beings have utilized the dried leaves and flowers (typically referred to as buds) of the nonpollinated female plant as an intoxicant. It's little wonder why. Most users report the marijuana high to be relaxing, relatively mild, and short in duration (anywhere from one to two hours). Best of all, unlike alcohol, the overindulgence in which can produce nausea, vomiting, hangovers, and even death in extreme circumstances, the use of marijuana produces very few negative side effects. Smoke too much and you'll most likely end up going to sleep.

Why Smoking Marijuana Gets You "High"

Believe it or not, scientists have only recently begun to discover the reasons why smoking pot gets you high. Today, researchers are just beginning to understand the many complex ways that marijuana— or more specifically, the various active chemicals of the plant— interacts with the human body.

The physical, therapeutic, and psychoactive effects one experiences after ingesting marijuana are derived primarily from a family of unique chemicals known as cannabinoids. We say "primarily" because there is emerging evidence that the plant's terpenes, a class of hydrocarbons found in the plant's essential oils, and flavonoids may also possess some mildly active therapeutic properties, but it appears that these components are far less active than cannabinoids. To date, investigators have identified over eighty distinct cannabinoids in the marijuana plant.[7] (Cannabinoids are typically concentrated in the resin produced by the plant's trichomes.) The most studied of these cannabinoids is delta-9-tetrahydrocannabinol, better known as THC. Why is this the most important of all the cannabinoids? Simple, THC is the stuff that gets you high!

Of the dozens of cannabinoids in marijuana, only THC is significantly psychoactive. Most other chemicals, such as cannabigerol (CBG) and cannabinol (CBN), possess mildly therapeutic properties but don't induce euphoria. Other compounds, most specifically the chemical cannabidiol (CBD), actually counteract some of the psychoactive effects of THC—acting as marijuana's "antimarijuana" mechanism.

Many of the effects of cannabis are dependent on the plant's THC content. Ingest a variety of marijuana that is high in THC (such as 10 or 15 percent THC) and you'll fairly quickly begin to feel its psychoactive effects, as well as a mild increase in heart rate. Consume a strain of marijuana that is grown for industrial purposes, which typically possesses less than 1 percent THC, and you'll feel no effects all.

(For the record, the average THC content of most domestic marijuana consumed in America hovers around 5 percent.[8])

Visit a legal medical marijuana "dispensary" (retail outlet) in California or a "coffee shop" in the Netherlands (where the sale of up to five grams of cannabis is legal to patrons over age eighteen) and you will discover a wide variety of marijuana strains to choose from, with names like "Blueberry," "White Rhino," and "Purple Kush." Like their names imply, these strains vary widely in appearance, aroma, flavor, THC content (and perhaps other cannabinoids), and price. Based on their chemical (cannabinoid) makeup, each strain also produces distinctive effects.

The physiological reasons a person experiences a high after ingesting marijuana is because the cannabinoids interact with individual receptors, so-called CB1 and CB2 receptors. The CB1 receptors, first identified in the late 1980s, are located primary in the brain and regulate the drug's psychoactive effects. The CB2 receptors, identified in the early 1990s, are located throughout the human body, and are responsible for many of the cannabinoids' more tangential therapeutic effects. (Naturally occurring chemicals in the human body that possess a similar molecular structure to herbal cannabinoids, so-called endocannabinoids, also interact with the CB1 and CB2 receptors to regulate many essential biological functions—including appetite, blood pressure, and reproduction.) Because the majority of the body's CB1 receptors are located in the frontal lobe region of the brain's cerebral cortex (which regulates emotional behavior) and the cerebellum (a region in the back of the brain that primarily controls motor coordination), but not the brain stem (which controls life-preserving functions like breathing), ingesting marijuana is not pharmacologically capable of causing a fatal overdose, regardless of THC potency. According to a 1995 report prepared for the World Health Organization (WHO), "There are no recorded cases of overdose fatalities attributed to cannabis, and the estimated lethal dose for humans extrapolated from animal studies is so high that it cannot be achieved by recreational users."[9]

The Physical and Psychological Effects of Marijuana

The specific psychological and physical effects experienced after consuming marijuana vary from person to person, and many of these effects are dependent on percentage of THC and other cannabinoids in the marijuana consumed. Moreover, new cannabis users tend to feel different effects compared with more experienced users. Sometimes the outcome is no effect at all (a phenomenon that seems to be limited to first- or second-time users only). However, if an inexperienced user consumes too much cannabis at one time, he or she may experience a mix of unpleasant physical and psychological feelings, such as a tachycardia (rapid heart beat), dry mouth, and a growing sense of paranoia. Fortunately these feelings, while mildly unpleasant, are only temporary and pose little-to-no actual long-term risk to the user's health.

As cannabis consumers become more experienced, their bodies become more tolerant to some of the drug's physical effects. Users also learn to better self-regulate (or "titrate") their dosage to avoid any dysphoric symptoms such as paranoia. As a result, most experienced marijuana consumers describe the cannabis high as a pleasant experience that helps them to relax or unwind. Many users claim that smoking marijuana makes them more talkative and outgoing in social situations, and many also say that the marijuana high enhances many of the body's senses, thus making activities like listening to music, watching a movie, or enjoying a home-cooked meal particularly enjoyable.

Different Ways of Consuming Marijuana

Cannabis is most often inhaled—either through a cigarette (joint), pipe, water pipe (also known colloquially as a "bong"), or vaporizer. Users tend to prefer inhalation as a route of administration because it enables them to experience marijuana's effects almost immediately after ingestion. This outcome allows consumers to moderate their dose fairly easily, taking a small number of "tokes" until they have achieved their ideal level of intoxication—similar to how most alcohol consumers sip wine or drink beer over the course of an evening.

Regardless of whether a person is inhaling cannabis via a joint, pipe, or bong, she is still subjecting her lungs to noxious smoke. Contrary to popular lore, the use of a water-pipe filtration system primarily cools marijuana smoke; the technology is not particularly efficient at eliminating the toxic by-products of combustion. In fact, one study found that bongs produce 30 percent more tar per cannabinoids than the unfiltered joint.[10] As a result, some cannabis consumers are now turning to vaporizers, devices that heat marijuana to a point where cannabinoid vapors form, but below the point of combustion. This technology, which we discuss further in chapter 5, allows users to enjoy the rapid onset of marijuana's effects while avoiding many of the associated respiratory hazards associated with smoking—such as coughing, wheezing, or chronic bronchitis.

Consuming moderate to high quantities of marijuana orally, such as in food or in a tincture (an oral alcohol-based solution), will yield a much different and often far more intense outcome. For starters, users will not begin to feel any psychoactive effects of the drug for a good forty-five to ninety minutes after ingestion, making it difficult to self-regulate the dosage. Once these effects do begin to take hold, they tend to be far stronger acting and last far longer (upwards of four to six hours is typical) than the effects of inhaled cannabis. This result is because of the way our bodies metabolize THC. When marijuana is smoked, THC passes rapidly from the lungs to the bloodstream and to the brain. By contrast, when marijuana is taken orally, a significant portion of THC is metabolized into the other chemicals, including the highly potent 11-hydroxy-THC, before reaching the brain. (Smoking cannabis produces only trace levels of this chemical.) As a result, both the physical and psychoactive effects of THC are magnified.

Of course, some users prefer these longer-lasting effects, just as some alcohol consumers prefer the stronger "buzz" of hard liquor over low-potency beer or wine. Other consumers, particularly less experienced users, prefer the milder effects associated with inhalation. Among users of medical marijuana, most favor inhaling cannabis as opposed to taking the legal oral pill Marinol because the prescription drug makes them feel "too stoned."

Why People Smoke Marijuana

According to U.S. government statistics, nearly 100 million Americans have tried marijuana and about 25 million have used it in the past year. So who are these people, and why do they break the law and risk arrest to smoke marijuana?

Readers can answer the first question by simply looking within their own social circle. Chances are you know someone who smokes or has smoked pot. Marijuana consumers include people from all walks of life, ethnic classes, and socioeconomic backgrounds (though, statistically, the demographic most likely to be current marijuana consumers are white males between the ages of eighteen and twenty-five). Barack Obama said that he smoked as a young man. He's hardly alone. Supreme Court Justice Clarence Thomas, former vice president Al Gore, and California governor Arnold Schwarzenegger all have admitted using marijuana at different times during their lives. We don't have nearly the space to begin listing all of the famous professional athletes and entertainers who use pot, but chances are that many of your favorite sports stars and celebrities do. In fact, a 2007 *New York Times* investigation estimated that up to 70 percent of pro basketball players engage occasionally or regularly in the use of marijuana.[11] Most likely at least a few of your colleagues at work enjoy an occasional toke, too. According to the U.S. government, most current marijuana users are gainfully employed.[12] Statistically, most marijuana users are also successful academically (overall academic performance is generally unaffected by cannabis use[13]) and financially. (At least one longitudinal study reports that increased marijuana use is associated with earning higher wages.[14]) Some former and current users, like Virgin-Atlantic Airways tycoon Sir Richard Branson, Progressive Auto Insurance founder Peter Lewis, and New York City mayor Michael Bloomberg, are even billionaires.

Surprisingly, little ethnographic research has been devoted to exploring the reasons that motivate so many people to use marijuana recreationally. United States government officials tend to argue that people use cannabis because they are addicted to it (an inflammatory charge that we address in detail in chapter 5). Others claim that people use marijuana because of "peer pressure" or because certain elements of the entertainment industry "glamorize" the drug's use. Predictably, the truth is far more ordinary.

Recently, investigators at the University of Alberta, Canada, conducted a series of lengthy interviews with male and female cannabis consumers. They found, not surprisingly, that the majority of adults who use cannabis recreationally do so to "enhance relaxation." They concluded: "[M]ost adult marijuana users regulate use to their recreational time and do not use compulsively. Rather, their use is purposively intended to enhance their leisure activities and manage the challenges and demands of living in contemporary modern society. Generally, participants reported using marijuana because it enhanced relaxation and concentration, making a broad range of leisure activities more enjoyable and pleasurable."[15]

In other words, people smoke marijuana recreationally for many of the same reasons people drink alcohol. In the following chapter we will consider whether these marijuana consumers—putting legal considerations aside—are making a rational choice to use marijuana, either consistently or occasionally, instead of alcohol.

chapter three

Removing the "Toxic" from Intoxication: An Objective Comparison of the Effects of Alcohol and Marijuana

The word *intoxicant* is derived from the Latin noun *toxicum* (poison). Today, this term is virtually synonymous with alcohol. (In fact, Merriam-Webster's online dictionary defines "intoxicate" as: "to excite or stupefy by alcohol.") The close association is appropriate, as the use of booze—particularly if it is not consumed in moderation—can cause an array of serious short-term and long-term health hazards, including cellular abnormalities, high blood pressure, cancer, organ damage, impaired judgment, and overdose death.

There are two primary reasons why the consumption of alcohol is so potentially harmful to health. The first is that alcohol acts primarily upon receptors and ion channels that, when stimulated, depress the inhibitory control mechanisms of the brain.[1] When low to moderate levels of alcohol are consumed, complex mental faculties such as memory, concentration, and judgment are affected, as well as one's mood and motor coordination. When a person ingests larger quantities of booze, lower brainstem centers are adversely affected. Since this region of the brain regulates cardiac and respiratory function, depression of this system may result in a loss of consciousness, breathing, or even death. Problematically, the amount of booze necessary to negatively affect these life-preserving functions is not much higher than the quantity most people would consume to relax recreationally. This relatively narrow safety margin explains why consumers of alcohol—such as young people engaged in competitive drinking games (where large amounts of booze are consumed in a short period of time)—accidentally overdose on the drug with frightening regularity.

The second reason why booze poses a danger to health is because its ingestion can have a toxic effect on many of the body's cells and major organs. Actually, it's not alcohol or even ethanol (the psycho-active ingredient in booze) per se that's responsible for these adverse effects, but rather the culprit is a little-known by-product known as acetaldehyde. After a person ingests alcohol, ethanol is metabolized to acetaldehyde, a carcinogenic substance that can cause a host of deleterious effects to cells and vital organs.[2] Because acetaldehyde is so potentially harmful to health, the body rapidly converts it to a nontoxic compound known as acetate, which is eventually broken down into carbon dioxide and water.[3] However, drinking too much alcohol at one time can impede the body's ability to properly break down acetaldehyde—the liver can typically only metabolize approximately one drink per hour—allowing the chemical to linger in the bloodstream. Over time, this toxic buildup may have adverse effects on many of the body's cells and major organs, including the heart, liver, breasts, and pancreas. In fact, a 2009 British study of some 1.3 million women age fifty to sixty-four reported that consuming as little as even one alcoholic beverage per day significantly elevated a female's risk of cancer, particularly breast cancer.[4] The study estimated that as many as 5 percent of all cancers diagnosed in women annually in the United States are likely the result of low to moderate alcohol consumption.

Of course, we are not providing this information in order to condemn the use of booze or to imply that the occasional consumption of moderate doses of alcohol is inherently damaging to the human body. Rather, our point is to illustrate the range of effects the widespread use of alcohol has on the health of the user and on society as a whole, and to compare these effects with those of marijuana. (In the interest of fairness, we explore several potential health risks associated with cannabis later in this chapter as well.) By providing this detailed analysis we hope that you, the reader, will better understand why we contend that the legalization and regulation of marijuana would provide adults with an option to use a safer and healthier alternative to their current recreational drug of choice, alcohol.

Drinking Alcohol in Moderation: Risks and Benefits

The moderate consumption of alcohol by otherwise healthy adults is typically a pleasurable, convivial, and relatively safe experience. In small doses, alcohol intake typically elevates the user's mood and reduces his or her anxiety. Drinking alcohol may also increase one's talkativeness and self-confidence, which is why many people choose to drink in bars, at family gatherings, or in other social situations.

According to most medical experts, the average male can consume up to two drinks per day and a nonpregnant, non-breastfeeding female can consume one drink daily without adversely affecting his or her health. The U.S. Center for Disease Control (CDC) defines a standard drink as either 12 ounces of beer, 8 ounces of malt liquor, 5 ounces of wine, or 1.5 ounces (a "shot") of distilled spirits or liquor. Because a woman's body contains less water than a man's, females are less able to dilute alcohol than are males. This is one reason why women tend to feel the psychoactive effects of the drug much faster than men.

Some limited data indicates that the regular consumption of low doses of alcohol may provide certain health benefits. For instance, red wine contains antioxidants that may assist in warding off heart disease, certain types of cancers, and Alzheimer's.[5] Drinking a pint of beer a day may be associated with stronger bones (the barley in beer contains silicon) and preventing osteoporosis.[6] A 2001 study published in the *Journal of the American Medical Association* reported that light and moderate drinkers were more likely to survive a heart attack compared to their nondrinking counterparts.[7] This result is likely because alcohol, like aspirin, affects blood coagulation and reduces blood clots. By contrast, drinking excessive amounts of alcohol may actually *promote* many of the conditions mentioned above, including increasing one's risk of high blood pressure, osteoporosis, heart attack, and stroke.

Of course, even drinking small amounts of alcohol can lower users' inhibitions and impair judgment. As few as one or two drinks can alter one's reaction time, decision making, and alertness—causing users to do or say something they may later regret, and putting them at an increased risk of having an accident. A 2006 University of Missouri study reported that the likelihood of experiencing an injury requiring hospitalization is "greatly increased" in the six hours immediately following the consumption of alcohol.[8] A separate 2009 study affirmed these results, finding, "Alcohol use in the six hours prior to injury was associated with [an elevated] relative risk compared with no alcohol use."[9] Predictably, alcohol use is a common cause of emergency-room admissions and workplace injuries.

Consuming larger quantities of alcohol in a short period of time will decrease muscle control and often increase the user's emotional instability. Drinking alcoholic beverages may also induce reckless behavior (this is why many drivers impaired by alcohol tend to drive faster than they would sober) and aggression (hence the popularity of the term "liquid courage"). After three (for a female) or four (for a male) drinks, a consumer's psychomotor skills are significantly impaired. Tragically each year, approximately 17,000 people die annually in drunk driving–related accidents.[10]

Alcohol consumption is closely associated with combative and violent behavior in both laboratory settings (clinical trials) and in public. We explain this association in detail in chapters 6 and 7, but for now here are just a couple factoids. According to government statistics, more than 40 percent of murderers in jail or state prison report that they had been drinking at the time of their offenses, and nearly one-half of those convicted of assault and sentenced to probation had been drinking when the offenses occurred.[11] Further, among those who have suffered an assault at the hands of an intimate partner, about two out of three say that alcohol played a role in the violent behavior.[12]

Drinking Alcohol in Excess

Consuming more than four drinks (for a female) or five drinks (for a male) in a short period of time is defined as binge drinking. In addition to the many adverse effects of alcohol listed above, binge drinking can also result in a hangover, nausea, blackouts, coma, brain damage, and death. The most severe of these ill effects are the result of alcohol's potent impact on the central nervous system.

Alcohol is categorized as a central nervous system depressant. As we explained at the beginning of this chapter, the consumption of too much alcohol at once can shut down the areas of the brain responsible for breathing and consciousness, causing the victim to pass out or, in the worst-case scenario, to die from asphyxiation. In fact, the severe vomiting associated with the overindulgence of alcohol is the body's way of trying to save itself when the brain recognizes that the consumer's blood-alcohol level is precipitously high. (The act of vomiting removes unabsorbed concentrations of ethanol from the stomach, which prevents the body's blood-alcohol level from spiking any higher.)

As is the case with many prescription medications, alcohol possesses a narrow window between what amounts may be consumed safely and what quantities may result in brain damage or death. For example, a 100-pound woman could imbibe one drink in an hour without suffering from virtually any adverse physical effects. However, were that same woman to consume nine times this dose of alcohol during the same time period (e.g., nine separate shots of vodka in sixty minutes), the outcome would likely be fatal.

Of course, alcohol's adverse effects on health are not limited simply to binge drinking. Studies have shown that the long-term heavy use of alcohol (e.g., more than two drinks per day for men or more than one drink per day for women) is linked to a host of deleterious health effects. In the book *Eating For Recovery: The Essential Nutrition Plan to Reverse the Physical Damage of Alcoholism* author Molly Siple writes that excessive alcohol use promotes angina, brain degeneration (for instance, a 2008 study reported that heavy drinking decreased total brain volume,[13] a condition that is associated with impaired learning and memory skills and dementia), ulcers, cirrhosis (alcohol abuse is responsible for more than 12,000 liver-related fatalities in the United States annually[14]), decreased testosterone production, compromised immunity, heart disease, hypertension, hypoglycemia, increased cancer risk, poor digestion, osteoporosis, pancreatitis (inflammation of the pancreas), psoriasis, and psychiatric disorders.[15] According to the National Institute on Alcohol Abuse and Alcoholism, the chronic use of booze is associated with approximately 35,000 deaths per year,[16] many of which are a direct result of the conditions listed above.

Further, alcohol consumption has been linked to both higher incidences of cancer as well as to the promotion of the spread of cancer. In pregnant women, the regular consumption of alcohol can cause serious harm to the health of the fetus. In females, too much alcohol can also negatively affect estrogen production and can disrupt menstruation. Booze is also high in calories (about seven calories per gram) and carbohydrates. This is why the consumption of alcohol (especially with meals) is sometimes associated with weight gain. Conversely, the more frequent use of alcohol has been linked in some instances with weight loss, particularly in women.[17] (Some experts believe that the heavy use of alcohol speeds up one's metabolism.)

Finally, the frequent consumption of beer, wine, or liquor can lead to alcohol dependence or alcoholism. According to the guidebook *Alcoholism: The Facts*, an alcoholic is defined as "a person who drinks, has problems from drinking, but goes on drinking anyway."[18] These problems may be the result of alcohol's impact on the user's physical health or the result of booze's impact on the user's behavior, interpersonal relationships, or emotional state of mind. The CDC presents a more specific definition, stating, "Alcoholism or alcohol dependence is a diagnosable disease characterized by several factors, including a strong craving for alcohol, continued use despite harm or personal injury, the inability to limit drinking, physical illness when drinking stops, and the need to increase the amount drunk to feel the effects."[19] According to population surveys, approximately 10 percent of U.S. citizens meet the criteria for problem drinkers; many of these people are likely battling alcoholism.[20] More disturbingly, as many as one in three Americans are believed to have suffered from an "alcohol use disorder" (such as sustained periods of binge drinking or alcoholism) at some point during their lives.[21]

Marijuana: Anything But Toxic

So, given the laundry list of adverse effects associated with a legal drug like alcohol, one would assume that the adverse effects of an illegal drug like marijuana must be far worse, right? Well, not exactly. Alcohol has set the bar far too high for that.

In 2004, investigators from the U.S. Centers for Disease Control wrote in the *Journal of the American Medical Association* (JAMA) that alcohol consumption is the third leading cause of death in America, trailing only tobacco smoking and poor diet.[22] By contrast, following a series of evidentiary hearings in 1988, the U.S. Drug Enforcement Administration's administrative law judge concluded, "In strict medical terms, marijuana is far safer than many of the foods we commonly consume. . . . Marijuana, in its natural form, is one of the safest therapeutically active substances known to man."[23]

Although cannabis is commonly referred to as a mild intoxicant (even by the authors of this book) there is, in fact, very little toxic about it—particularly when compared to the effects of ethanol. In moderate and even heavy doses, cannabinoids are virtually nontoxic to healthy cells and human organs.

Moreover, as we mentioned in chapter 2, compounds in marijuana actually mimic the body's own neuromodulators (the endocannabinoids), which are essential to maintaining homeostasis, good health, and perhaps even protecting the body from many of adverse health effects associated with old age.[24] This discovery has led some experts to theorize that the use of cannabis may, in some cases, supplement the endocannabinoid system and, in turn, help to moderate certain diseases[25] and maintain optimum health.

As noted already, unlike alcohol, ingesting cannabis cannot cause a lethal overdose, nor is its use, even long-term, associated with higher levels of mortality. According to a 1997 study by Kaiser Permanente of over 65,000 people, lifetime marijuana use "showed little if any effect . . . on non-AIDS mortality in men and total mortality in women."[26] (Authors noted that the increased risk of AIDS mortality in men was not because of a causal relationship, but arguably because patients with late-stage HIV/AIDS were more likely to be using cannabis for symptomatic relief than other males in the cohort.) A separate study of this population found no association between pot use and increased risks of developing tobacco-use related cancers.[27] In fact, no cases of lung cancer were identified among subjects who used marijuana but did not smoke tobacco. (For more information regarding marijuana smoking and cancer risk, please see chapter 5.) A previous review of cannabis use and mortality risk in a cohort of 45,540 Swedish conscripts reported that marijuana smokers had no higher risk of death compared to nonusers, after investigators controlled for subjects' social backgrounds.[28]

The use of marijuana, contrary to the consumption of alcohol, is not associated with increased incidents of injury. The same University of Missouri investigators who in 2006 reported that drinking alcohol significantly increased one's risk of accident requiring hospitalization also determined that marijuana use was associated "with a substantially decreased risk of injury."[29] Additionally, Swiss investigators in 2009 reported that people who consumed cannabis had a lower risk of injury compared to those who consumed no drugs or alcohol.[30]

Marijuana use is seldom regarded as a cause of violent behavior, traffic injury, or damage to the brain. (All of these subjects are explored in detail in chapter 5.) Though not advised, the use of marijuana by pregnant mothers appears to have far less impact on the fetus than the use of alcohol, which has been linked to permanent and severe birth defects. (Cannabis use among pregnant mothers has been associated with lower birth weight and, in a handful of studies, cognitive differences in young children[31]—though this finding remains controversial and inconclusive.) Marijuana use, even over the long term, also fails to induce the sort of physical cravings and withdrawal symptoms associated with booze. (Please see chapter 5 for a full discussion of this subject.) At worst, marijuana-associated "withdrawal" is described by the U.S. National Academy of Sciences as "mild and subtle."[32] By contrast, the withdrawal symptoms from alcohol are so physically severe that they can lead to delirium tremens, which may be fatal.

But what about the claim that marijuana is more dangerous to the body than alcohol because cannabinoids and their by-products are fat soluble (and thus exit the fat cells slowly) while alcohol is water soluble and exits the body more quickly? As noted previously, cannabinoids are surprisingly nontoxic, so their persistence in the body poses no serious threat to health. In fact, it's this slow half-life that likely prevents cannabis users from suffering from substantial abstinence symptoms (e.g., physical withdrawal) when they cease using it.[33] Marijuana's excretion pattern is hardly unique. Plenty of other legal drugs, such as certain prescription steroids, are fat soluble and have similarly slow elimination times. About the only serious downside of pot's pharmacokinetics is that its metabolites (a type of by-product) can be detected on certain drugs tests—primarily hair tests and urinalysis—for days and sometimes weeks after past use, making cannabis consumers far more susceptible to discrimination in the workplace. By contrast, most other drugs—including booze, cocaine, and methamphetamine—are only detectable on standard drug screens for a period of hours.

The Medical Benefits of Cannabis

Cannabis possesses a variety of therapeutic applications. Most of you reading this book are undoubtedly familiar with some of the ways that marijuana can provide symptomatic relief. After all, pot's prowess as an appetite stimulant has been a source of late-night comedy sketches for decades now. (Yes, smoking marijuana will give you "the munchies." Of course, if you're suffering from severe weight loss due to HIV, AIDS, cancer chemotherapy, or cachexia, the munchies is a life-saving side effect—not a laughing matter.) You are also likely aware of the use of cannabis to treat severe nausea—inhaling pot reduces the "gag reflex"—and glaucoma, an eye disorder characterized by abnormally high pressure within the eyeball. (Smoking marijuana temporarily reduces intraocular pressure.) And we're pretty sure all of you know that marijuana can elevate mood and alleviate anxiety.

Some of you may have also heard that cannabis can reduce involuntary muscle spasms and incontinence, symptoms commonly associated with multiple sclerosis and other movement disorders. Marijuana can also induce sleep, alleviate the tics associated with Tourette's syndrome, and significantly reduce inflammation and pain, particularly neuropathy (a type of nerve pain that's notoriously difficult to treat with standard analgesics). A 2007 study conducted at San Francisco General Hospital concluded that smoking cannabis reduced HIV-associated sensory neuropathy in patients by more than 30 percent. "Smoked cannabis was well tolerated and effectively relieved chronic neuropathic pain from HIV-associated neuropathy," scientists reported in the journal *Neurology*.[34]

Chances are that far fewer of you are aware that cannabis's medical utility extends far beyond treating just the symptoms of disease. In some cases, it appears that marijuana can effectively treat disease itself. For instance, marijuana possesses strong antioxidant properties that can protect the brain during trauma and potentially ward off the onset of certain neurological diseases such as Alzheimers.[35] In fact, in one of the great political ironies, the U.S. Department of Health and Human Services holds a patent—it's patent no. 6630507—on the use of cannabinoids as antioxidants and neuroprotectants.[36] That's right, the same government that classifies cannabis as a Schedule I illicit drug (which under federal law is defined as possessing "no currently accepted medical use in treatment") owns the intellectual property rights to several of the plant's naturally occurring, therapeutic chemicals!

The long-term use of cannabinoids appears to slow the progression of certain neurological and autoimmune diseases such as multiple sclerosis. In clinical trials, MS patients taking Sativex (an oral spray consisting of natural, whole-plant cannabis extracts) for a period of several years report requiring *fewer* daily doses of the drug to effectively treat their pain and spasticity.[37] Because multiple sclerosis is a progressive disease, conventional wisdom dictates that patients should be taking more doses, not fewer, over time to attain the same relief. Writing in the journal *Brain*, British researchers concluded, "Cannabis may also slow the neurodegenerative processes that ultimately lead to chronic disability in multiple sclerosis and probably other diseases."[38]

Preclinical reports also indicate that cannabis may moderate the progression of amyotrophic lateral sclerosis (a.k.a. Lou Gehrig's Disease), a fatal neurodegenerative disorder, and at least one study demonstrated that the administration of THC both before and after the onset of ALS halted disease progression and prolonged survival in mice.[39] Would pot have this same effect in humans? For that answer, all one has to do is ask Cathy Jordan—a colleague of one of the authors of this book.

Cathy has lived with ALS longer than almost anyone in America— an accomplishment she credits almost entirely to her use of cannabis. Diagnosed with the disease in 1986, Cathy was given only years to live (more than half of ALS patients die within three years after the onset of symptoms). Between 1986 and 1989, doctors prescribed Cathy a steady stream of muscle relaxants and mood-altering narcotics. Despite her steady diet of pharmaceuticals, neither Cathy's condition nor her mood improved. By the late 1980s, she became despondent and wanted to die. And then a friend suggested she try cannabis.

The therapeutic effects of Cathy's first marijuana cigarette were both immediate and profound. Cannabis dramatically alleviated her pain and relaxed her muscles, while simultaneously stimulating her appetite and elevating her mood. Within years Cathy had abandoned virtually all of her conventional medications in favor of cannabis, and her doctors—as well as those of us who know her—have been stunned by the results. "It's exciting to see the doctors pass out," she joked to a Florida newspaper in 2008. "They're just miffed that I'm so healthy."[40]

Finally, studies have also shown that cannabinoids can prevent the onset of diabetes[41] and can limit the spread of multidrug-resistant infections such as MRSA, more commonly known as "the Superbug."[42] (According to the *Journal of the American Medical Association*, MRSA is responsible for nearly 20,000 hospital-stay-related deaths annually.) Marijuana also has profound cancer-fighting abilities. In laboratory settings, the controlled administration of cannabinoids selectively targets and kills malignant cancer cells associated with gliomas (brain cancer), prostate cancer, breast cancer, lung cancer, skin cancer, pancreatic cancer, and lymphoma.[43] Writing in the prestigious journal *Nature*, Spanish researcher Manuel Guzman reported: "Cannabinoids inhibit tumor growth in laboratory animals. They do so by modulating key cell-signaling pathways, thereby inducing direct growth arrest and death of tumor cells, as well as by inhibiting tumor angiogenesis and metastasis. Cannabinoids are selective antitumor compounds, as they can kill tumor cells without affecting their non-transformed counterparts."[44] Troublingly, a review of the scientific literature reveals that U.S. investigators first reported on the prolific anticancer properties of cannabis more than thirty years ago—in 1974![45] Yet to date, the U.S. government has never commissioned one single follow-up study assessing the potential of cannabis to treat this deadly disease.

Should Certain People Avoid Marijuana?

Of course, like alcohol, marijuana poses certain risks and is not for everyone. Consuming cannabis will alter mood, influence emotions, and temporarily alter perception, so users should always pay particular attention to their set (emotional state) and setting (environment) prior to using it. The drug should not be taken prior to driving, or prior to engaging in tasks that require certain learning skills, such as the retention of new information. (In other words, don't consume marijuana before attending class or taking an exam.) Adolescents should also be advised to avoid cannabis, as it remains unclear whether marijuana, like alcohol, adversely affects the developing brain.[46] Pregnant women should also avoid cannabis, just as they should avoid consuming tobacco or booze. Men trying to start a family may also wish to refrain from marijuana, as heavy use has been shown to lower sperm count and motility in preclinical, though not human, trials.[47]

Because inhaling smoke over long periods of time is typically associated with increased incidences of cough, wheezing, and bronchitis, inhaling cannabis (or any substance) ought to be avoided by people suffering from various breathing-related issues, such as chronic obstructive pulmonary disease, also known as COPD. (However, unlike tobacco smoke, cannabis smoke acts as a bronchodilator,[48] which is why it is sometimes used by those with asthma without ill effects.) Consuming cannabis can also temporarily increase heart rate, and likely should not be advised for people suffering from high blood pressure or a history of heart disease.[49] There is also data indicating that patients suffering from severe liver problems should avoid using marijuana regularly, as some studies have identified a positive association between daily pot use and the progression of liver fibrosis (excessive tissue build up) and steatosis (more commonly known as fatty liver disease) in select patients with hepatitis C.[50] (Other studies have reported that cannabis may be helpful for those with the disease.[51])

Adults who suffer from so-called addictive personality disorders may wish to avoid marijuana, as they may possess greater tendencies to become dependent upon the drug. That said, as we discuss in detail in chapter 5, far more people statistically become dependent on booze than ever exhibit symptoms of drug dependence from pot.

Finally, there's evidence—though not conclusive—indicating that people suffering from mental illness, such as psychosis, depression, or schizophrenia, or who have a family history of mental illnesses, should avoid cannabis. To date, a handful of studies have identified an association, albeit a minor one, between chronic cannabis use and increased symptoms of mental illness.[52] (Other studies have failed to find such a link.[53]) However, interpretation of this data is troublesome. First, people with certain mental illnesses, such as schizophrenia, tend to use *all* intoxicants in greater percentages than the general public. Second, confounding factors such as poverty, family history, and polydrug use make it difficult, if not impossible, for researchers to adequately determine whether any cause-and-effect relationship exists between cannabis use and mental illness. Notably, there is no available evidence indicating that cultures whose populations engage in the widespread use of marijuana suffer greater incidences of mental illness compared to populations that rarely use it.

Consequently, many experts believe that pot's alleged association with mental illness, if there truly is one, may be due to patients' self-medicating with cannabis. Survey data and anecdotal reports of individuals finding therapeutic relief from both clinical depression and schizotypal behavior are common within medical lore, and clinical testing on the use of cannabinoids to treat certain symptoms of mental illness has been recommended.[54] That said, we still believe that individuals who may be predisposed to such conditions should exercise caution before engaging in the use of cannabis.

Pot vs. Alcohol: What Do the Experts Say?

We expect that some readers will be tempted to disregard or discount the analysis in this chapter, based on an assumption that we have skewed the data in order to advance our political agenda. For that reason, we have decided to close this discussion of the relative risks and dangers posed by the use of cannabis and alcohol by summarizing the views of experts who have also reviewed this issue. Let's see what they have to say.

In the mid-1990s, the World Health Organization commissioned a team of scientists to compare the health and societal consequences of cannabis use compared to other drugs, including alcohol, nicotine, and opiates. After comparing and quantifying the magnitude of dangers associated with these drugs, the researchers concluded: "Overall, most of these risks [associated with marijuana] are small to moderate in size. In aggregate they are unlikely to produce public health problems comparable in scale to those currently produced by alcohol and tobacco. . . . On existing patterns of use, cannabis poses a much less serious public health problem than is currently posed by alcohol and tobacco in Western societies."[55] The WHO ultimately removed these findings from its final 1997 report, "Cannabis: A Health Perspective and Research Agenda," after allegedly receiving political pressure from the United States, which argued that such conclusions could undermine its ongoing criminal prohibition of marijuana.[56]

French scientists at the state medical research institute INSERM published a similar review in 1998. Researchers categorized legal and illegal drugs into three distinct categories: those that pose the greatest threat to public health, those that pose moderate harms to the public, and those substances that pose little to no danger. Not surprisingly, alcohol, heroin, and cocaine were placed in the most dangerous category, while tobacco and hallucinogens were categorized as posing moderate risks to the public's health. Investigators determined that cannabis posed the least danger to public health.[57]

In 1989, a research advisory panel for the state of California reviewed the health effects of pot and alcohol. They concluded, "[A]n objective consideration of marijuana shows that it is responsible for less damage to the individual and to society than are alcohol and cigarettes."[58] Predictably, the state's attorney general refused to publicly release the report.

In 2002, a special Canadian senate committee completed an exhaustive review of marijuana and health, finding that "scientific evidence overwhelmingly indicates that cannabis is substantially less harmful than alcohol and should be treated not as a criminal issue but as a social and public health issue."[59] Senators concluded their report by calling for the legalization of cannabis to consumers age sixteen and older, a request that was subsequently ignored by the majority of Parliament.

In 2007, the Australian Institute of Health and Welfare hired a team of scientists to assess the impact of alcohol, tobacco, and other drugs on public health. Predictably, researchers found that the consumption of alcohol was a significant contributor to death and disease. "Alcohol harm was responsible for 3.2% of the total burden of disease and injury in Australia," they concluded. "Of the 14 risk factors examined, alcohol was responsible for the greatest amount of burden in males under the age of 45."[60] By comparison, cannabis use was responsible for zero deaths and only 0.2 percent of the estimated total burden of disease and injury in Australia.

That same year, a team of experts conducted a similar review for the esteemed British medical journal the *Lancet*. After evaluating the physical and social harms of numerous legal and illegal drugs, the authors determined that alcohol posed far greater health and safety risks than cannabis.[61]

Finally, in 2008 a team of researchers commissioned by the non-partisan British think tank the Beckley Foundation published a report assessing marijuana's risk to health. They concluded: "The public health impact of contemporary patterns of cannabis use are modest by comparison with those of other illicit drugs (such as the opioids) or with alcohol. In the former case this reflects the absence of fatal overdose risk from cannabis. In the latter case, it reflects the much lower risks of death from cannabis than alcohol-impaired driving, fewer adverse effects on health, lower rates of regular use to intoxication for cannabis than for alcohol, and the lower rate of persistence of cannabis use into older adulthood."[62] The report's authors ultimately recommended, as do we, that the public's health and safety would best be served by amending federal drug control laws to allow for the sale and use of cannabis in a manner similar to alcohol.

PART TWO

Choice, Interrupted

chapter four

"Reefer Madness" and All That Jazz: The Origins of Pot Prohibition

Given everything you've read in chapter 3, chances are many of you are wondering: "So how on Earth did we get here? Why is it that our state and federal laws embrace alcohol—a drug that is a known cause of a frightening array of adverse health effects and behaviors—while criminalizing the use of marijuana, which is seldom associated with such problems?"

Good question. After all, it wasn't always like this. Throughout most of America's history, marijuana and alcohol were both legal. In 1920, the federal government decided to outlaw booze, yet members of Congress had yet to enact *any* legal restrictions on the consumption of cannabis. However, by the 1930s the political climate had changed dramatically. In 1933, the Twenty-first Amendment was ratified, repealing alcohol prohibition. Yet just four years later, on August 2, 1937, President Franklin Roosevelt signed the Marihuana Tax Act into law, ushering in a new form of prohibition—one that remains with us to this day.

So what the hell happened?

The Tide Turns

For the first three hundred years of our nation's history American farmers cultivated cannabis—then known exclusively as either "hemp" or "Indian hemp"—for its cordage fiber content. Some historians believe that colonists harvested America's first hemp crop in 1611 near Jamestown, Virginia. Shortly thereafter, The British Crown ordered settlers to engage in wide-scale hemp farming[1]—a practice that continued in earnest up until the turn of the twentieth century. Even into the early part of the 1900s, the United States Department of Agriculture extolled the virtues of hemp as a high-yield, low-maintenance crop.[2] At that time, Americans no more considered the plant to be a recreational drug than someone today would label corn or soy an intoxicant. Domestically grown cannabis possessed very little THC content and was not consumed recreationally. In fact, the term *marijuana* was not yet a part of the American lexicon.

In addition to its industrial uses, much of the public was also familiar with the plant's utility as a medicine. While practicing in India in the early 1800s, Irish physician William O'Shaughnessy first began documenting the medical uses of cannabis, which he later introduced into Western medicine in 1839. By the 1850s, the preparation of oral cannabis extracts became available in U.S. pharmacies, where they remained a staple for the next sixty years.[3] Typically these products were marketed under the plant's alternative botanical name, *cannabis indica*. (Unlike industrial varieties of the crop that were grown domestically, pharmaceutical supplies of cannabis were often imported from other countries, like India.[4]) Despite the drug's widespread availability as a medicine, reported recreational abuses of cannabis were virtually nonexistent in the literature of that time. In fact, during Congressional hearings leading up to the passage of the Harrison Narcotics Act of 1914—the nation's first federal antidrug act—witnesses argued *against* prohibiting cannabis, stating that "as a habit forming drug its use is almost nil."[5] Congress heeded their advice and excluded marijuana from the statute.

By the early 1920s, however, public and political acceptance of cannabis had changed significantly. The plant's popularity as both a commercial crop and folk remedy was on the wane, as competing commercial products like cotton-based textiles and opiate-based medications began to gain a wider share of the market. At the same time, newspapers and law enforcement personnel, primarily in the American Southwest, began reporting on the use of a new, highly dangerous "narcotic" called *marijuana* (or as it was typically spelled then, *marihuana*). From the papers' and police officers' salacious accounts of the drug's purported effects, it's unlikely that most Americans had any idea that the so-called "loco weed" and cannabis hemp were actually one and the same.

The Rise of "Reefer Madness"

Aside from infrequent accounts of hash smoking by East Indian and Lebanese immigrants, there is little, if any, evidence that the recreational use of marijuana had any cultural foothold in America prior to the influx of Mexican laborers in the early 1900s.[6] However, the Mexicans' custom of smoking the flowering tops of the female plant almost immediately drew concern from public officials and law enforcement—who alleged that inhaling the drug empowered users with "superhuman strength and turned them into bloodthirsty murderers."[7]

As early as 1913, a handful of cities and states in the American south began prohibiting the use of marijuana, and by the early 1920s, numerous western states—including California, Colorado, Nevada, Texas, Utah, and Wyoming—had outlawed possessing pot.[8] In many of these states, the public rationale for this crackdown was as racially motivated as it was transparent: "All Mexicans are crazy, and this stuff (referring to marijuana) is what makes them crazy."[9] Other regions of the country followed suit—including many states that had virtually no Mexican immigrant population and virtually no reported incidents of marijuana use to speak of—arguing that legislation was necessary to preemptively stop the spread of "the Devil's Weed" before it reached their borders.

By the late 1920s, lurid newspaper headlines and editorials promoting the alleged dangers of marijuana began sweeping the nation. This excerpt, taken from a July 6, 1927, *New York Times* story, epitomizes the content and tone of much of the reporting of this era:

Mexican Family Go Insane
Five Said To Have Been Stricken By Eating Marihuana

A widow and her four children have been driven insane by eating the Marihuana plant, according to doctors, who say there is no hope of saving the children's lives and that the mother will be insane for the rest of her life.

. . . Two hours after the mother and children had eaten the plants, they were stricken. Neighbors, hearing outbursts of crazed laughter, rushed to the house to find the entire family insane. Examination revealed that the narcotic marihuana was growing among the garden vegetables.[10]

The public's concern over the supposed marijuana menace grew, and in 1930 Congress responded by establishing the Federal Bureau of Narcotics (FBN). Selected to head this new agency was a "law and order" evangelist named Harry J. Anslinger. For the next three decades, Anslinger would single-handedly dictate U.S. drug policy. Many of his highly sensationalized views on weed linger in the public mind to this day.

Beginning in the mid-1930s, Anslinger and the FBN launched an unprecedented (for the time) media campaign warning Americans of the alleged perils of pot. By this time, the drug's use was not only popular among Mexican immigrants, but it had also become vogue among certain segments of the African American community, most notably southern jazz musicians. The Bureau warned that smoking marijuana inspired blacks and Hispanics to commit rape and engage in other acts of uninhibited violence. "His sex desires are aroused and some of the most horrible crimes result," one widely disseminated FBN news bulletin reported. "He hears light and sees sound. To get away from it, he suddenly becomes violent and may kill."[11] Seizing upon many white Americans' preexisting racial prejudices, Anslinger often emphasized that these alleged acts of violence were primarily directed toward Caucasian women.

Anslinger further claimed that Mexican "dope peddlers" frequently offered free samples of marijuana cigarettes to children on their way home from school. "Parents beware! Your children . . . are being introduced to a new danger in the form of a drugged cigarette, marijuana," Anslinger warned in a prominent FBN radio address. "Young [people] are slaves to the narcotic, continuing addiction until they deteriorate mentally, become insane, [and] turn to violent crime and murder."[12]

Possessing a flair for the theatrical, Anslinger bragged about keeping a "gore file" consisting of outrageous, unsubstantiated, and sometimes fraudulent newspaper stories that detailed pot's supposedly mind-altering and behavioral effects. One such account read, "While under the influence of the drug, the subject thrust his hand through his hair, and found that his fingers passed through his crackling skull and into his warm, cheesy brain."[13]

Predictably, Anslinger's and the FBN's antipot diatribes fueled national headlines and prompted legislative action. By 1935, most states in the country had enacted laws criminalizing the possession and use of pot, and newspaper editors were frequently opining in favor of stiffer and stiffer penalties for marijuana users. As Anslinger's rhetoric became prominent, he found additional allies who were willing to carry his crusading message to the general public. Among these were the Women's Christian Temperance Union and the Hearst newspaper chain—the latter of which luridly editorialized against the "insidious and insanity producing marihuana" in papers across the country.[14]

Members of state and local law enforcement also joined the FBN's antimarijuana crusade. Writing in *The Journal of Criminology*, Wichita, Kansas, police officer L. E. Bowery asserted that the cannabis user is capable of "great feats of strength and endurance, during which no fatigue is felt." Bowery's overwrought screed, which for years thereafter would be hailed by advocates of prohibition as the definitive "study" of the drug, concluded: "Sexual desires are stimulated and may lead to unnatural acts, such as indecent exposure and rape. . . . [Marijuana use] ends in the destruction of brain tissues and nerve centers, and does irreparable damage. If continued, the inevitable result is insanity, which those familiar with it describe as absolutely incurable, and, without exception ending in death."[15]

The Marihuana Tax Act

By 1937, Congress—which had resisted efforts to clamp down on the drug some two decades earlier—was poised to act, and act quickly, to enact blanket federal prohibition. Ironically, by this time virtually every state had *already* ratified laws against cannabis possession. Nonetheless, local authorities argued that the marijuana threat was so great that federal intervention was also necessary.

On April 14, 1937, Representative Robert L. Doughton of North Carolina introduced House Bill 6385, which sought to stamp out the recreational use of marijuana by imposing a prohibitive tax on the drug. The measure was the brainchild of the U.S. Treasury Department, and mandated a $100 per ounce tax on the transfer of cannabis to members of the general public. Interestingly, a separate antimarijuana measure introduced that same year sought to directly outlaw possession and use of the drug. However, this proposal was assumed at that time to have been beyond the constitutional authority of Congress.

Members of Congress held only two hearings to debate the merits of Doughton's bill. The federal government's chief witness, Harry

Anslinger, told members of the House Ways and Means Committee that "traffic in marijuana is increasing to such an extent that it has come to be the cause for the greatest national concern. . . . This drug is entirely the monster Hyde, the harmful effect of which cannot be measured."[16] Other witnesses included a pair of veterinarians who testified that dogs were particularly susceptible to marijuana's effects. "Over a period of six months or a year (of exposure to marijuana), . . . the animal must be discarded because it is no longer serviceable," one doctor testified.[17] This would be the extent of "scientific" testimony presented to the committee.

The American Medical Association (AMA) represented the most vocal opposition against the bill. Speaking before Congress, the AMA's legislative counsel Dr. William C. Woodward challenged the legitimacy of the alleged "Demon Weed."

> We are told that the use of marijuana causes crime. But yet no one has been produced from the Bureau of Prisons to show the number of prisoners who have been found addicted to the marijuana habit. An informal inquiry shows that the Bureau of Prisons has no evidence on that point.
>
> You have been told that school children are great users of marijuana cigarettes. No one has been summoned from the Children's Bureau to show the nature and extent of the habit among children. Inquiry of the Children's Bureau shows that they have had no occasion to investigate it and know nothing particularly of it.
>
> . . . Moreover, there is the Treasury Department itself, the Public Health Service. . . . Informal inquiry by me indicates that they have no record of any marijuana or cannabis addicts.[18]

Woodward further argued that the proposed legislation would severely hamper physicians' ability to utilize marijuana's therapeutic potential. While acknowledging that the drug's popularity as a prescription medicine had declined, Woodward nonetheless warned that the Marihuana Tax Act "loses sight of the fact that future investigations may show that there are substantial medical uses for cannabis."[19]

Woodward's criticisms of the bill's intent—as well as his questions regarding whether such legislation was objectively justifiable—drew a stern rebuke from the chairman of the committee. "If you want to advise us on legislation, you ought to come here with some constructive proposals, rather than criticism, rather than trying to throw obstacles in the way of something that the federal government is trying to do," the AMA's counsel was told. "Is not the fact that you were not consulted your real objection to this bill?"[20]

Despite the AMA's protests, the House Ways and Means Committee approved House Bill 6385. House members even went so far as to elevate Anslinger's propaganda to Congressional findings of fact, stating: "Under the influence of this drug the will is destroyed and all power directing and controlling thought is lost. . . . [M]any violent crimes have been and are being committed by persons under the influence of this drug. . . . [S]chool children . . . have been driven to crime and insanity through the use of this drug. Its continued use results many times in impotency and insanity."[21]

Anslinger made similar horrific pronouncements before members of the Senate, which spent even less time debating the measure than did the House. By June, less than three months after the bill's introduction, the House of Representatives voted affirmatively to pass the proposal, which was described by one congressman as having "something to do with something that is called marijuana. I believe it is a narcotic of some kind."[22]

Weeks later, after the Senate had approved its version of the bill, the House was asked to vote once again on the measure. Prior to the House's final vote, one representative asked whether the American Medical Association had endorsed the proposal, to which a member of the Ways and Means Committee falsely replied that the

AMA's "Dr. Wharton [sic]" had given the measure his full support.[23] Following this brief exchange of *inaccurate* information, Congress gave its final approval of the Marihuana Tax Act without a recorded vote.

President Franklin Roosevelt promptly signed the legislation into law. The Marihuana Tax Act officially took effect on October 1, 1937—thus setting in motion the federal government's foray into the criminal enforcement of marijuana laws that continues to this day.

Richard Nixon, the Controlled Substances Act, and the "War on Drugs"

Had the passage of the Marihuana Tax Act of 1937 succeeded in permanently stamping out the recreational use of pot, none of you would be reading this book right now. Of course, as we all know, the lid could only be kept on the pot for so long. In the mid-1960s— some thirty years after the passage of federal pot prohibition—a whole new generation of young people, mostly college-aged students, began altering their consciousness with marijuana. Some viewed the use of cannabis as a rejection of "the establishment" and the culture of their parents' generation. Others viewed marijuana consumption as a form of political protest and civil disobedience against U.S. foreign policy in Vietnam. And some simply discovered that they preferred the relaxing and conscious-expanding effects of marijuana over alcohol.

This explosion of pot use in the 1960s was quickly followed by a proportional rise in pot arrests—which ballooned from just over 10,000 a year in the early part of the decade to more than 100,000 per year by the end of the decade.[24] Most of those arrested faced severe penalties, including mandatory sentences of several years to, in some cases, *decades*, in jail.

As marijuana arrests and prosecutions swelled, those convicted were no longer limited primarily to ethnic minorities like African

Americans and Hispanics—the groups state and federal politicians had initially targeted decades earlier. Predictably, as more white, middle-class, otherwise law-abiding young people were "caught up in the system," politicians began facing increasing pressure to review their multi-decade-long pot policies. Many state legislators began revamping their marijuana laws—reducing simple pot possession offenses from felonies to criminal misdemeanors. By 1970 even members of Congress felt compelled to act.

Following a series of hearings in 1969, during which experts estimated that between eight and twelve million Americans were likely using the drug recreationally, Congress passed the Controlled Substances Act of 1970. This comprehensive legislation eliminated mandatory minimum drug sentences—Congress eventually reinstated them in the 1980s, reduced pot penalties, and established federal "scheduling" criteria for illicit and licit substances.

Of the five schedules established under the United States Controlled Substances Act, the most restrictive was dubbed "Schedule I." Drugs classified in the Schedule I category, like heroin and LSD, remained prohibited under all circumstances because they, by law, were defined to possess "no currently accepted medical use," "a high potential for abuse," and "a lack of accepted safety."

In 1970, members of Congress begrudgingly categorized marijuana as a Schedule I drug, but with a caveat: the classification was only supposed to be temporary! That's because the Controlled Substances Act also called for the creation of a special federal commission to study all aspects of the cannabis plant, its use, and its users. Once and for all, Congress was going to determine whether there was any truth to the claims that pot was a dangerous drug deserving of strict prohibition.

After nearly two years of scientific study, Congress' marijuana commission—known as the National Commission on Marihuana and Drug Abuse—completed its investigation. The multimillion-dollar study was trumpeted as "the most comprehensive study of marihuana ever made in the United States."

The commission's report, entitled *Marihuana: A Signal of Misunderstanding*, was issued to Congress and President Richard Nixon on March 22, 1972. In clear and unambiguous language, it rebutted virtually every negative claim that politicians and members of law enforcement had ever made about the drug's alleged dangers. It reported:

> Looking only at the effects on the individual, there is little proven danger of physical or psychological harm from the experimental or intermittent use of the natural preparations of cannabis. . . . Marihuana clearly is not in the same chemical category as heroin insofar as its physiologic and psychological effects are concerned. In a word, cannabis does not lead to physical dependence. . . . The incidence of psychiatric hospitalizations for acute psychoses and of use of drugs other than alcohol is not significantly higher than among the non-using population. . . . These findings are somewhat surprising in view of the widespread belief that cannabis attracts the mentally unstable, vulnerable individual.
> . . . The fact should be emphasized that the overwhelming majority of marihuana users do not progress to other drugs.
> . . . [N]o substantial evidence existed of a causal connection between the use of marihuana and the commission of violent or aggressive acts. . . . [R]ather than inducing violent or aggressive behavior through its purported effects of lowering inhibitions, weakening impulse control and heightening aggressive tendencies, marihuana was usually found to inhibit the expression of aggressive impulses by pacifying the user.[25]

Speaking before Congress, the commission's chairperson, Republican governor Raymond P. Shafer of Pennsylvania, concluded,

"The recommendations of the Commission . . . is that we do not feel that private use or private possession (of marijuana) in one's own home should have the stigma of criminalization [and] that the people who experiment (with marijuana) should not be criminalized for that particular behavior."[26] This policy recommendation, known as "decriminalization," called for Congress to eliminate all criminal penalties punishing the private possession of cannabis, as well as those restricting nonprofit transactions of the drug. In place of these penalties, the commission suggested that Congress impose sanctions of no more than a nominal fine for the use and possession of marijuana. The commission further recommended that cannabis no longer be classified as a Schedule I drug under federal law.

While some in Congress were willing to take the commission's findings under advisement, President Nixon immediately made it clear that he would do no such thing. Privately, legend has it that he tossed the report in the trash without ever reading it. Publicly, he took to the airwaves to announce, "I shall continue to oppose efforts to legalize marijuana."[27]

In fact, in the months following the publication of the Shafer report, Nixon did the exact *opposite* of what the commission had recommended. Flexing the federal muscle of the newly formed anti-crime "super-agency," the U.S. Drug Enforcement Administration, Nixon announced that his administration was launching the first official "war" on drugs. Public enemy number 1? You guessed it: marijuana. Under Nixon's watch, annual marijuana-related arrests rose from 119,000 in 1969 (when Nixon took office) to 445,000 in 1974 (when he resigned from office).[28] And the war on pot still rages today.

chapter five

Reality Check: The Truth Behind Common Marijuana Myths

As we discussed in chapter 4, the origins of cannabis prohibition were steeped in prejudice, misinformation, and fear mongering. Inflammatory accusations against marijuana and marijuana consumers were typically unsubstantiated, while evidence refuting these claims often went ignored. Troublingly, nearly one hundred years later, little has changed.

Today, the U.S. government and many law enforcement officials continue to justify the need for cannabis prohibition by promoting alarmist myths that distort the truth about marijuana. Some of these distortions, such as the claim that pot smoking is linked to violent and psychotic behavior, date back to the "Reefer Madness" era of the 1930s. Other myths, like the claim that today's cannabis is highly addictive, are more recent yet equally specious. Nonetheless, this propaganda serves as the basis for the criminal prohibition of marijuana today.

Therefore, what we intend to do in this chapter is to provide you with an advanced course in the truth about marijuana. In the pages that follow, we will dispel some of the more prominent myths about cannabis by providing sound scientific, health, criminal justice, and economic data. We hope that you will keep these facts in mind the next time you hear government officials spreading lies about cannabis.

MYTH: Today's marijuana is significantly stronger and thus more dangerous than the marijuana of the past.

> "We're no longer talking about the drug of
> the 1960s and 1970s. This is Pot 2.0."[1]
> — *John P. Walters, U.S. drug czar (2001–8)*

> "This ain't your grandfather's or your father's marijuana.
> This will hurt you. This will addict you. This will kill you."[2]
> —*Mark R. Trouville, U.S. Drug Enforcement*
> *Agency chief (DEA Miami division)*

FACT: The potency of today's cannabis is only slightly higher, on average, than the pot of twenty or thirty years ago. Marijuana's increased potency, however, is not associated with increased health risks.

As best we can interpret it, the implication of the myth of increased pot potency is that the marijuana of past generations was impotent enough to have rendered it largely innocuous—unless of course you were Mexican or African American, in which case it made you violent, insane, and sexually deviant. In fact, those of you reading this who experimented with weed twenty, thirty, or forty years ago *didn't* actually get high; the 1960s and '70s were all just a population-wide placebo effect—or so the "not your father's marijuana" crowd claims.

Prohibitionists argue that today's marijuana is so strong that it will literally blow your mind. Never mind that police and lawmakers made these same dire claims about the suddenly not-as-dangerous-as-we-once-said-it-was pot of the 1960s and '70s. This time, they *really* mean it.

So what does the science say? Is today's pot, on average, significantly stronger than the cannabis that was available some ten, twenty, or thirty years ago? And if so, does this increase in potency make it more harmful to one's health?

According to marijuana-potency data compiled annually the University of Mississippi at Oxford—which has been randomly testing seized samples of cannabis for THC content since the late 1970s—the average amount of THC in domestically produced marijuana is around 5 percent. By comparison, the average THC content of marijuana during the 1980s, as reported by UMiss, hovered around 3 percent.[3] (The federal government did not consistently test the strength of marijuana prior to this time, and the small number of samples that were assessed during the late 1970s were primarily sampled from dried Mexican "kilobricks" of atypically low potency.[4]) Does this increased potency equate to an increased safety risk? Not at all.

As we explained previously, THC—regardless of potency—is virtually nontoxic to human cells or organs, and is incapable of causing a fatal overdose. Currently, doctors prescribe Marinol, a legal prescription medication that is *100 percent* synthetic THC, and nobody at the drug czar's office seems overly concerned about its health effects. (Nobody at the U.S. Food and Drug Administration is particularly concerned either. In 1999, FDA officials downgraded Marinol from a Schedule II controlled substance to a Schedule III drug—a change made largely because of its low abuse potential and impeccable safety record.)

Furthermore, survey data gleaned from cannabis consumers in the Netherlands—where users may legally purchase pot of known quality—indicates that most cannabis consumers prefer less potent pot,[5] just as the majority of those who drink alcohol prefer beer or wine rather than 190 proof Everclear or Bacardi 151. When consumers encounter unusually strong varieties of marijuana, they adjust their use accordingly and smoke less.

Specifically, a 1989 John Hopkins University study reported that marijuana users readily differentiate between varying strengths of pot, taking "smaller puff and inhalation volumes and shorter puff duration for the high marijuana dose compared to the low dose."[6] A 2007 University of California study assessing cannabis users' pot intake reaffirmed this conclusion.[7] In short, the stronger the herb, the less smoke consumers inhale into their lungs. You'd think the drug czar would be celebrating.

MYTH: Using marijuana will inevitably lead to the use of "harder" drugs like cocaine and heroin.

> "Marijuana is a gateway drug. In drug law enforcement,
> rarely do we meet heroin or cocaine addicts who did
> not start their drug use with marijuana."[8]
> —*Karen Tandy, U.S. DEA administrator (2005–7)*

FACT: The overwhelming majority of marijuana users never try another illicit substance.

Predictably, Ms. Tandy neglects to mention that virtually everyone who has ever used cannabis tried tobacco and alcohol first. Of course, it is not our intention to imply that alcohol and cigarettes are any more culpable than pot for driving folks to hard drug use. I believe, however, that it is important to state for the record that, sequentially, virtually all people dabble in the use of these two intoxicants prior to ever experimenting with marijuana. Yet it is hard to imagine that even the most ardent prohibitionist would argue that this sequential correlation would justify criminally prohibiting the use of booze or tobacco by adults.

As for the rest of Ms. Tandy's assertion, it should come as no surprise that the minority of people who use highly dangerous drugs like heroin or crack cocaine have previously used the far more popular and safer drug marijuana. But despite pot's popularity—more than four in ten adults have tried it according to the federal government—Americans' use of other illicit substances remains comparatively low. For example, data provided by the U.S. Department of Health and Human Services indicates that only 3.5 percent of U.S. citizens have ever tried crack, and fewer than 2 percent of Americans have ever tried heroin.[9] As for cocaine, the next most commonly used illicit drug in America after cannabis, fewer than 15 percent of Americans have tried it.[10]

But what about those minority of cannabis users who *do* go on to use other illicit drugs? Isn't the pot to blame? Not at all. In fact, experts generally identify "environmental circumstances," not the prior use of a drug, as the primary reason why a handful of people transition from the use of marijuana to harder drugs. As noted in a report published by the Netherlands Institute of Mental Health and Addiction:

> As for a possible switch from cannabis to hard drugs, it is clear that the pharmacological properties of cannabis are irrelevant in this respect. There is no physically determined tendency towards switching from marijuana to harder substances. Social factors, however, do appear to play a role. The more users become integrated in an environment ("subculture") where, apart from cannabis, hard drugs can also be obtained, the greater the chance that they may switch to hard drugs. Separation of the drug markets is therefore essential.[11]

Or, to put it another way: If U.S. policymakers legalized marijuana in a manner similar to alcohol—thereby allowing its sale to be regulated by licensed, state-authorized distributors rather than by criminal entrepreneurs and pushers of various other, hard drugs—the likelihood is that *fewer*, not more, marijuana smokers would ever go on to try any another illicit substance. In short, it is marijuana prohibition, not the use of marijuana itself, that functions as a gateway to the potential use of harder drugs.

MYTH: Marijuana is highly addictive. Millions of Americans seek treatment every year because they become dependent upon marijuana.

> "Marijuana is a much bigger part of the American addiction problem than most people ... realize. There are now more teens going into treatment for marijuana dependency than for all other drugs combined."[12]
> —*John P. Walters, U.S. drug czar (2001–8)*

FACT: Marijuana lacks the physical and psychological dependence liability associated with other intoxicants—including tobacco and alcohol. Very few cannabis users voluntarily seek drug treatment for pot "addiction." The majority of marijuana smokers in drug treatment were arrested for pot possession and ordered into treatment as a condition of their probation.

Is cannabis addictive? All of us have probably known at least one person in our lives who we thought "smoked too much pot." But there is certainly a difference between doing something too much (in the opinion of others) and being addicted. Are marathoners "addicted" to running? Are Red Sox season ticket holders "addicted" to baseball? Putting aside these analogies for a moment, let's look at what the science tells us. Numerous reports, including one by the prestigious British medical journal the *Lancet* and another cited in the *New York Times*, have found cannabis's risk of physical or psychological dependence to be mild compared to most other drugs, including alcohol and tobacco. In fact, two experts in the field—Drs. Jack E. Henningfield of the U.S. National Institute on Drug Abuse and Neal L. Benowitz of the University of California at San Francisco—reported to the *New York Times* that pot's addiction potential is no greater than caffeine's.[13]

Pot's relatively low risk of dependency was affirmed by the nonpartisan National Academy of Sciences Institute of Medicine, which published a comprehensive federal study in 1999 assessing marijuana's impact upon health. Its authors determined, "[M]illions of Americans have tried marijuana, but most are not regular users [and] few marijuana users become dependent on it." The researchers added, "[A]lthough [some] marijuana users develop dependence, they appear to be less likely to do so than users of other drugs (including alcohol and nicotine), and marijuana dependence appears to be less severe than dependence on other drugs."[14]

How less likely? According to the 267-page report, fewer than 10 percent of those who try cannabis ever meet the clinical criteria for a diagnosis of "drug dependence" (based on DSM-III-R criteria). By contrast, investigators reported that 32 percent of tobacco users, 23 percent of heroin users, 17 percent of cocaine users, and 15 percent of alcohol users meet the criteria for "drug dependence."[15]

But what about the oft-repeated claims that more people are in drug treatment for pot than for all other drugs combined? As usual, the devil is in the details. According to published statistics, up to 70 percent of all Americans enrolled in drug "treatment" for cannabis were ordered there by the criminal justice system.[16] By no definition are these people "addicts" in any literal sense of the word. According to 2006 statistics provided by the U.S. government Substance Abuse Mental Health Services Association (SAMHSA), more than one-third of those in treatment for pot *hadn't even used the drug* in the thirty days prior to admission.[17] Rather, they are average Americans who have experienced the misfortune of being busted for possessing a small amount of weed who are forced to choose between rehab or jail. Yet, prohibitionists disingenuously claim that these admission rates justify the need to continue arresting pot users—even though they are well aware that it is America's marijuana *policy*, not marijuana use—that is fueling the surge in drug treatment.

MYTH: Smoking cannabis is more harmful to health than smoking tobacco and causes lung cancer.

"Someone who smokes marijuana regularly may have many of the same respiratory problems that tobacco smokers do. . . . Marijuana has the potential to promote cancer of the lungs and other parts of the respiratory tract because marijuana smoke contains 50 percent to 70 percent more carcinogenic hydrocarbons than does tobacco smoke."[18]

—*U.S. Drug Enforcement Administration*

FACT: Smoking cannabis is not associated with higher incidences of lung cancer or any other types of cancer. Compounds in marijuana may even be protective against the spread of various forms of cancer.

Okay, first the bad news. Inhaling noxious smoke of any kind, including cannabis smoke, isn't good for you. Like tobacco smoke, marijuana smoke contains levels of select polycyclic aromatic hydrocarbons (though, unlike the DEA claims, most of these agents are present in marijuana smoke at levels *lower* than those found in cigarette smoke.)

Now for the good news. Cannabis consumers can greatly reduce or eliminate their consumption of most, if not all, of these unwanted elements by engaging in vaporization rather than smoking. Cannabis vaporization heats marijuana to a temperature where active cannabis vapors form, but below the point of combustion—therefore enabling consumers to significantly reduce their intake of gaseous combustion toxins, including carbon monoxide. In 2007, a team of investigators at San Francisco General Hospital in California compared the combustible contents of smoked marijuana cigarettes to pot vapors. They determined: "Vaporization of marijuana does not result in exposure to combustion gases and [was] preferred by most subjects compared to marijuana cigarettes. . . . [It] is an effective and apparently safe vehicle for THC delivery."[19]

Of course, most marijuana consumers don't have access to a vaporizer. In fact, federal and statewide prohibitions outlawing the use of so-called drug paraphernalia make the use and possession of marijuana vaporizers illegal in most places. So then, is the average pot smoker at risk for developing cancer?

The answer to this question, as of this writing, appears to be no. Unlike tobacco smoking, marijuana inhalation has not been positively associated with increased incidences of cancers of the lung, mouth, upper aerodigestive tract (e.g., pharynx, larynx, or esophagus), breast, colon, skin, or prostate.[20]

In 2006, the results of the largest case-controlled study ever to investigate the respiratory effects of marijuana smoking reported that pot use was not associated with lung-related cancers, even among subjects who reported smoking more than 22,000 joints over their lifetime.[21] "We hypothesized that there would be a positive association between marijuana use and lung cancer, and that the association would be more positive with heavier use," the study's lead researcher, Dr. Donald Tashkin of the University of California at Los Angeles, told the *Washington Post*. "What we found instead was no association at all, and even a suggestion of some protective effect" among marijuana smokers who had lower incidences of cancer compared to nonusers of the drug.[22]

MYTH: Smoking marijuana impairs driving in a manner that is worse than alcohol. Marijuana consumption is responsible for tens of thousands of traffic accidents every year.

"The extent of the problem of marijuana-impaired driving is startling. . . . Marijuana smoking [has] disastrous effects . . . on driving."[23]
—*Karen Tandy, U.S. DEA administrator (2005–7)*

FACT: Marijuana intoxication appears to play, at most, a minor role in traffic injuries.

While it is well established that alcohol consumption increases motor vehicle accident risk, evidence of marijuana's culpability in on-road driving accidents and injury is nominal by comparison.

That's not to say that smoking marijuana won't temporarily impair psychomotor skills. Given a strong enough dose, it most certainly will. However, pot's psychomotor impairment is seldom severe or long lasting, and variations in driving behavior after marijuana consumption are noticeably *less* pronounced than the impairments exhibited by drunk drivers.

Unlike motorists under the influence of alcohol, individuals who have recently smoked pot are aware of their impairment and try to compensate for it accordingly, either by driving more cautiously or by expressing an unwillingness to drive altogether.[24] As reported in a 2008 Israeli study assessing the impact of marijuana and alcohol on driving performance, "[S]ubjects seemed to be aware of their impairment after THC intake and tried to compensate by driving slower; alcohol seemed to make them overly confident and caused them to drive faster than in control sessions."[25]

A previous report by Toronto's Centre for Addiction and Mental Health reached a similar conclusion, finding: "[S]ubjects who have received alcohol tend to drive in a more risky manner. The more cautious behavior of subjects who have received marijuana decreases the impact of the drug on performance, whereas the opposite holds true for alcohol."[26]

Of course, none of this information is meant to imply that smoking marijuana makes you a "safe" driver. Smoking marijuana can alter driving performance. In closed-course and driving-simulator studies, marijuana's acute effects on driving include minor impairments in tracking (eye-movement control) and reaction time, as well as variation in lateral positioning, headway (drivers under the influence of cannabis tend to follow less closely the vehicle in front of them), and speed (as previously noted, drivers tend to decrease speed following cannabis inhalation).[27] Moreover, a handful of studies have reported a positive association between very recent cannabis exposure and a gradually increased risk of vehicle accident, though this increased risk is far lower than the risk presented by the consumption of even small amounts of alcohol.

For example, a 2007 case-control study published in the *Canadian Journal of Public Health* reviewed ten years of U.S. auto-fatality data. Investigators found that U.S. drivers with blood alcohol levels of .05, a level *below* the legal limit for intoxication in the United States, experienced an elevated crash risk that was more than *three times higher* than individuals who tested positive for marijuana.[28] A prior review of auto accident fatality data from France reported similar results, finding that drivers who tested positive for *any* amount of alcohol had a *four times greater* risk of having a fatal accident than did drivers who tested positive for marijuana.[29] Both studies noted that, overall, few traffic accidents appeared to be attributed to a driver's operating a vehicle while impaired by cannabis.

To summarize, a motorist who has just smoked marijuana is a safer driver than one who has just consumed alcohol (even quantities of alcohol that are well within the legal limit for drinking and driving in most countries), but he or she is arguably not a "safe" driver. As with alcohol or most over-the-counter cold remedies, cannabis consumers are best advised to abstain from operating a motor vehicle for several hours after imbibing, and they should always designate at least one person to act as a sober designated driver.

MYTH: Smoking marijuana causes permanent damage to the brain.

> "Long-term effects of using marijuana include 'burnout'...
> and permanent damage to thinking skills"
> —*Syndistar/Fox Pro Media antidrug educational pamphlet*[30]

FACT: Marijuana use by adults—even long-term, heavy use of the drug—has, at most, only a negligible residual impact on cognition and memory skills.

Of all of the myths surrounding marijuana use, the allegation that smoking pot will cause permanent brain damage is the most pervasive. Yet there is little-to-no scientific evidence to substantiate it.

Unlike alcohol, marijuana use—even heavy use—appears to have, at most, only "subtle" effects on brain development.[31] In 2009, investigators at San Diego State University and the University of California at San Diego reported:

> Recent research has indicated that adolescent substance users show abnormalities on measures of brain functioning, which is linked to changes in neurocognition over time. Abnormalities have been seen in brain structure volume, white matter quality, and activation to cognitive tasks, even in youth with as little as one to two years of heavy drinking and consumption levels of 20 drinks per month, especially if [more than] four or five drinks are consumed on a single occasion. Heavy marijuana users show some subtle anomalies too, but generally not the same degree of divergence from demographically similar non-using adolescents.[32]

Further, in adults cannabis consumption is not associated with residual deficits in cognitive skills, as measured by magnetic resonance imaging, neurocognitive performance testing, or functional magnetic resonance imaging.

For example, Harvard Medical School researchers performed magnetic resonance imaging on the brains of long-term cannabis users (reporting a mean of 20,100 lifetime episodes of smoking) and controls (subjects with no history of cannabis use). Imaging displayed "no significant differences" between heavy marijuana smokers compared to nonsmokers.[33]

Additional clinical trials have reported similar results. An October 2004 study published in the journal *Psychological Medicine* examined the potential adverse effects of marijuana on cognition in monozygotic male twins. It reported "an absence of marked long-term residual effects of marijuana use on cognitive abilities."[34] Likewise, a 2002 clinical trial published in the *Canadian Medical Association*

Journal determined, "Marijuana does not have a long-term negative impact on global intelligence."[35]

Though a handful of studies have reported that current marijuana users sometimes score slightly lower than nonusers on certain cognitive tests, these same studies also report that cannabis consumers score the same as nonusers once they have abstained from the drug for several days or weeks. Notably, a 2001 study published in the journal *Archives of General Psychiatry* found that long-term cannabis smokers who abstained from the drug for one week "showed virtually no significant differences from control subjects (those who had smoked marijuana less than 50 times in their lives) on a battery of 10 neuropsychological tests." Investigators further added, "Former heavy users, who had consumed little or no cannabis in the three months before testing, [also] showed no significant differences from control subjects on any of these tests on any of the testing days."[36]

Far from damaging the brain, it appears that many of the active components in marijuana may, in some instances, actually be good for it. Scientific studies indicate that pot's ingredients can prevent against brain damage due to stroke, traumatic brain injury, and ironically enough, alcohol poisoning.[37] Recently, researchers at the University of Saskatchewan in Saskatoon, Canada, reported that the administration of synthetic cannabinoids in rats stimulated the proliferation of newborn neurons (nerve cells) in the hippocampus region of the brain. The results stunned investigators, who noted that virtually all other psychoactive substances—including alcohol, cocaine, nicotine, and opiates—*suppress* rather than promote neurogenesis. "This is quite a surprise," team investigator Xia Zhang told the Canadian newspaper the *Globe and Mail*. "Chronic use of marijuana may actually improve learning memory when the new neurons in the hippocampus can mature in two or three months."[38]

MYTH: Smoking marijuana is linked to violence and psychotic behavior.

> "Boy on Skunk Cannabis Butchered Grandmother"
> "Cannabis Drove Brighton Man to Kill Himself"
> "Cannabis Users Risk Their Sanity"
> —*Assorted British tabloid newspaper headlines
> between 2007–8, as compiled by the authors*

FACT: Smoking cannabis does not cause the user to engage in violent or delinquent behavior. Marijuana does not appear to be a cause of mental illness in otherwise healthy individuals.

If you think the headlines above were plucked from 1937, think again. Yes, it's true: some myths never die.

Despite decades of anecdotal claims, no credible research has shown marijuana use to be a causal factor in violence, aggression, or delinquent behavior. As concluded by the National Commission on Marihuana and Drug Abuse, "[M]arihuana is not generally viewed by participants in the criminal justice community as a major contributing influence in the commission of delinquent or criminal acts."[39]

More recently, a 2002 Canadian Special Senate Committee review affirmed: "Cannabis use does not induce users to commit other forms of crime. Cannabis use does not increase aggressiveness or anti-social behavior."[40] By contrast, research has demonstrated that certain legal drugs, such as alcohol, do induce aggressive behavior.

"Cannabis differs from alcohol . . . in one major respect. It does not seem to increase risk-taking behavior," the British Advisory Council on the Misuse of Drugs concluded in 2002. "This means that cannabis rarely contributes to violence either to others or to oneself, whereas alcohol use is a major factor in deliberate self-harm, domestic accidents and violence."[41]

More recently, a logistical retrogression analysis of approximately nine hundred trauma patients by SUNY-Buffalo's Department of Family Medicine reported that use of cannabis is not independently associated with either violent or nonviolent injuries requiring hospitalization.[42] Alcohol and cocaine use were associated with violence-related injuries, the study found. Accordingly, fewer than 5 percent of state and local law enforcement agencies in the United States identify marijuana as a drug that significantly contributes to violent crime in their areas.[43]

Attempts to link marijuana use and the development of mental illness in otherwise healthy adults are equally specious. A comprehensive review by the British Advisory Council on the Misuse of Drugs determined, "The evidence for the existence of an association between frequency of cannabis use and the development of psychosis is, on the available evidence, weak."[44] Additionally, a 2005 University of Oxford meta-analysis regarding cannabis use and its impact on mental health reported that marijuana smoking, even over the long term, will not cause "any lasting physical or mental harm. . . . Overall, by comparison with other drugs used mainly for 'recreational' purposes, cannabis could be rated to be a relatively safe drug."[45]

In short, smoking pot won't make you crazy—that is, unless you're the drug czar or the head of the DEA, in which case all bets are off.

chapter six

How Society Is Systematically Driving Us to Drink

"I will learn from these mistakes, train hard
and make you proud again."
—MICHAEL PHELPS, FEBRUARY 2009

Dateline: February 1, 2009. It's Super Bowl Sunday and throughout the nation millions of Americans have stocked their shelves and refrigerators with alcohol for the big game. In living rooms across the country, guests will enjoy the libations and gawk at the humorous beer commercials sprinkled liberally throughout the telecast. Like the Fourth of July and fireworks, the Super Bowl and booze are an American tradition. There is no societal stigma associated with this excessive drinking. It is all part of the celebration. Like the old saying goes: "We don't have a drinking problem. We drink. We get drunk. No problem."

But as the day's festivities build to a climax, the nation is thrown into turmoil. Internet headlines announce that Olympic swimming hero Michael Phelps, who months earlier had electrified audiences throughout the world by winning eight gold medals in Beijing, had been captured in full digital glory taking a bong hit at a private party. The horrors! How could he do such a thing?

Almost immediately online articles appear, replete with quotes of disillusionment from anyone with even a tangential connection to the world's most decorated Olympian. Hours later, Phelps issues a public statement. He apologizes for his "regrettable" behavior and "bad judgment," and promises "it will not happen again." Was Phelps's apology issued because he was reportedly also drunk and "obnoxious" at the same party? Of course not. Being drunk in public is not the sort of behavior that triggers public outrage and social condemnation. Taking a hit or two of marijuana, on the other hand, most certainly is.

In the days that followed, our society piled on the way it often does when someone famous is caught smoking grass. Predictably, there was mockery and derision. For example, one Huffington Post blogger posted a column with the headline, "Phelps Congratulates Cardinals on Super Bowl Win."[1] (The Arizona Cardinals lost the game on a last-minute touchdown, caught, ironically enough, by another recently outed marijuana smoker, Pittsburgh Steelers wide receiver Santonio Holmes.) The body of the essay included such "witticisms" as Phelps claiming to have missed the end of the game because of a "wicked attack of the munchies." Naturally, the writer did not mock Phelps's drunken behavior.

Several of Phelps's corporate sponsors, while not immediately jumping off the financial gravy train, expressed their own sense of dismay. Michael Humphrey, chief executive of the PureSport beverage company, issued the following statement: "We applaud the fact that he (Michael Phelps) has taken full and immediate responsibility for his mistake and apologized to us, his fans and the public and we support him during this difficult time." Similarly, a U.S. congressman from Phelps's home state of Maryland, Elijah Cummings, appeared on television to express his deep concern and disappointment in this otherwise "great kid."

By week's end, America's corporate establishment brought the hammer down upon Phelps. First, the Kellogg's Company dropped the Olympic gold medalist as a spokesperson, explaining that his behavior was "not consistent with the image of Kellogg." Soon thereafter, USA Swimming, the sport's national governing body, suspended Phelps from competition for three months—even though he had *not* violated any existing drug-testing policy. (Marijuana is not a prohibited substance during the off-season.) "[W]e decided to send a strong message to Michael," the organization said, "because he disappointed so many people, particularly the hundreds of thousands of USA Swimming member kids who look up to him as a role model and a hero."

Far from being outraged (at least publicly) about the decision, Phelps was contrite and repentant. According to USA Swimming, Phelps "voluntarily accepted this reprimand" and was "committed to earn[ing] back [their] trust."[2]

As if all of this wasn't enough, Leon Lott, the sheriff in Richland County, South Carolina, where the bong hit heard round the world had occurred, launched a criminal investigation of the matter worthy of a hunt for a suspected terrorist. Several weeks following the incident, twelve armed deputies, with guns drawn, burst into the home where the party had taken place and arrested two residents. Cops also seized four laptops, a desktop computer, and an electronic storage device. They found less than six grams of marijuana in the home—which is about what they would find in any off-campus apartment in the United States—but they were hardly concerned about illegal contraband. Rather, the lawyers for the defendants said that the cops *only* wanted to know whether the two individuals had witnessed Phelps using marijuana. Richland County law enforcement officials later arrested six more individuals, all in an effort to weed out the nation's most famous weed aficionado. Finally, after several weeks of this taxpayer-funded silliness, Sheriff Lott eventually announced that he had failed to find sufficient evidence to press criminal charges against Michael Phelps, or for that matter, anyone else.

Let's review, shall we? The most successful Olympian in history attends a college party, pounds a few beers, and allegedly behaves like a drunken ass. At some point during the evening, he inhales a bit of marijuana. When all of this becomes public, he is run through the social, corporate, and legal wringer—but only for his suspected pot use. So what lesson has our champion swimmer learned? That's simple. Next time he goes out in public, he should just stick to being drunk and obnoxious.

———

Michael Phelps's story is hardly unique. Rather, it highlights the myriad ways that society intentionally steers citizens away from cannabis and toward the use of a more harmful substance, alcohol.

Sure, all Americans know that marijuana is illegal, and most are aware that the government purposely spreads misleading information about the drug's allegedly adverse effects. But how many of you have stopped to think about the ways that other entities are directly or indirectly involved in maintaining cannabis prohibition? After all, the government could not uphold the status quo all by itself. It requires the assistance of private and public employers, athletic associations, and the mainstream media. Each of these groups, by acting according to (assumed) societal norms, their leaders' own personal biases, or perhaps, as we discuss later, their own financial interests, take actions that reinforce the government's criminalizing of cannabis.

For example, USA Swimming was under no legal or ethical obligation to suspend Phelps from athletic competition. It did so solely to "send a strong message." In other words, the organization's leaders used their authority to impose a subjective standard of moral conduct. They did not assert this power to discourage Phelps's arguably irresponsible use of alcohol (nor, for that matter, did they say a word when he was photographed grabbing some ass in the Playboy Club in Las Vegas a few months prior). Instead, they reserved their punishment for Phelps's use of an herb that is less detrimental to athletic performance than alcohol.

Of course, some of you reading this book may believe that the actions taken by USA Swimming, Kellogg's, and the mainstream media were appropriate because, after all, marijuana *is* illegal. That's true, but consider this: Would these entities have reacted similarly if Phelps had received a traffic violation? Of course not. Yet in roughly a dozen states, small-scale pot possession is treated no differently under the law than a speeding ticket. Moreover, in Phelps's case, his actions did not even rise to the level of a prosecutable offense! No, let's be clear here. This blowback had little to do with Phelps "breaking the law," and had everything to do with Phelps behaving "unacceptably."

For over thirty-five years, prohibitionists have waged a cultural battle against marijuana use in the United States. Yet, as we explained in chapter 1, cannabis has remained exceedingly popular in spite of these efforts. Perhaps because of this continued popularity, opponents of marijuana use—both in government and the private sector—have, in recent years, redoubled their efforts and employed new and diverse tactics to try to deter the public from using cannabis. While these coercive actions and public policies have certainly not eliminated the drug from our society, there is little doubt that *collectively* they have produced an artificially low level of marijuana use among U.S. adults.

If You Can't Beat 'Em, Arrest 'Em

The most overt way that our society attempts to discourage marijuana use is by the strict enforcement of prohibition. The personal possession of even small amounts of marijuana for nonmedical purposes is currently illegal in all fifty states (except Alaska), with penalties ranging widely from the imposition of small fines to extensive jail time. However, the mere fact that pot possession is illegal under the law does not tell the complete story. Just because an activity is defined as a crime does not necessarily mean the police will aggressively target and prosecute offenders. For example, in many states adultery is illegal, but you don't see cops staking out "no-tell motels" looking to crack down on adults who engage in a little extramarital fun on the side. The police don't get to choose which laws exist, but they—and the local officials and police chiefs that guide them— have an incredible amount of latitude to determine which ones they will enforce vigorously. And they have decided that they *love* arresting marijuana users.

From the time Nixon officially launched the federal war on drugs to today, law enforcement agencies have busted nearly twenty million Americans for pot-related offenses, mostly for simple possession.[3] And in recent years, the annual number of arrests have been rising. According to the FBI's Uniform Crime Reports, in 1994 police made 402,717 marijuana possession arrests. Just three years later, in 1997, they made over 600,000 pot possession arrests. But even that annual total wasn't enough. From the years 2000 to 2003, police averaged 641,000 marijuana-possession arrests per year; from 2004 to 2007 the average was a whopping 723,612 arrests!

Yet you will rarely, if ever, hear America's top cops or politicians bragging about law enforcement's propensity for busting pot smokers. For instance, George W. Bush's drug czar, John Walters, speaking at a press conference in 2008, proclaimed that nobody goes to jail for marijuana possession. "Finding somebody in jail or prison for first-time, non-violent offender for possession of marijuana is like finding a unicorn," Walters said. "It doesn't exist."[4] First of all, this assertion simply isn't true. In fact, the Marijuana Policy Project disproved Walter's allegation with a quick Google search.[5] But let's give the former drug czar the benefit of the doubt. Let's acknowledge that many people arrested for marijuana possession are not ultimately sentenced to serve time in prison. Does that mean these "offenders" get off scot-free? Hardly.

For starters, even in states where marijuana possession is decriminalized—meaning, there is generally no risk of jail time associated with the offense—those caught with a small amount of pot must still pay fines, appear in court, and may still receive a lifelong criminal record. In most other states, first-time offenders receive probation and must undergo months of mandatory drug testing. If they fail any of these court-mandated drug tests, as many eventually do, they *will* be sentenced to prison.

In addition, with the growing popularity of drug courts, marijuana defendants—especially young people—face the very real threat of being forced to attend so-called drug-treatment programs. As we noted in chapter 5, up to 70 percent of Americans enrolled in state drug-treatment programs for cannabis have been placed there by the courts. Are these people struggling with an addiction to pot? No, not at all. In fact, many of these individuals had not even used marijuana in the month prior to their admission—a strong indication that they did not have a serious addiction to the substance.

Of course, beyond the very real risk of fines, probation, and court-ordered drug treatment, a marijuana arrest and conviction, even if it does not result in jail time, can produce additional collateral damage. Individuals unfortunate enough to experience pot-related run-ins with law enforcement also face, depending on where they live, the likelihood of losing their driver's license (even if the offense did not involve the operation of a motor vehicle), their job, their kids, their home (particularly if they reside in publicly subsidized housing), their student financial aid, their right to vote, their ability to adopt children, and even their food stamps. Believe it or not, virtually no other criminal offenses—including violent crimes like rape or murder—trigger this same plethora of sanctions. Even an armed bank robber remains eligible for federal financial aid following his conviction.

And while it does not appear, at least on the surface, that the aggressive enforcement of marijuana laws has significantly lowered cannabis-use rates in the United States, one can be certain that the threat of legal repercussions has influenced more than a few Americans, older Americans especially, to forego pot and choose booze instead. Citing his own personal history with marijuana and alcohol, *St. Louis Post-Dispatch* opinion columnist Bill McClellan emphasized this point in a 2009 column, writing:

I consider pot no more harmful than booze. Maybe less harmful. . . . Of course, in a perfect world, we wouldn't need any intoxicants. We'd all be high on life, digging sunsets.

But few of us have found that kind of inner peace, and so we seek something less natural than a sunset. For most of us, it's a drink to take the edge off the day. For others, it's a joint.

The odd thing is one is legal and one isn't. I say odd because I have enjoyed many a drink and many a joint, and I don't feel any better about myself because I no longer smoke pot. I no longer smoke pot only because I don't want to get in trouble. In that regard, I'm no different than most of my contemporaries.[6]

Passing the Test

As shocking as America's running marijuana arrest tally is, the reality is that the long arm of the law only extends so far. For example, the fear of arrest does not likely come into play when you're enjoying a dinner party with friends and someone breaks out a joint. Chances are the police are not going to break down the door, catch you in mid puff and haul you away (or issue you a citation). Yet there is still a very good chance that many of you reading this book—even if you enjoy using marijuana—will take a pass instead of a hit. The reason: drug testing.

Although no public opinion poll has ever asked why many adults who might otherwise consume marijuana choose to abstain instead, we know from firsthand experience—as do many of you—that the specter of drug testing is a primary reason. Today, many jobs and schools impose random drug testing. In most cases, just one positive test for marijuana can cause serious consequences, including suspension from school or dismissal from employment. For those subjected to these drug-testing programs, it doesn't matter that a private toke is highly unlikely to lead to an arrest. The real threat of punishment looms in the days and weeks afterward.

As we explained in chapter 3, drug testing is especially pernicious for marijuana consumers because THC's by-products are detectable on standard drug screens (typically urinalysis) for longer periods of time than are other illicit substances. Because marijuana's primary by-product, the carboxy THC metabolite, is fat soluble, it can often remain detectable in urine for several days after the drug is consumed. For regular users of cannabis, carboxy THC may remain detectable on a urine drug screen for several weeks, or even months, after use. By contrast, evidence of past cocaine or heroin use is no longer detectable on a urine screen after a couple of days. In other words, an employee who enjoys a line or two on Friday night can rest assured that his or her job will still be secure the following Monday. But if that same employee smokes marijuana over the weekend and is randomly drug tested the following week, chances are he or she will find him- or herself in the unemployment line. As a result many potential marijuana users are forced to avoid the substance at *all* times, since a random drug test could be right around the corner. Needless to say, those who choose to drink alcohol after work live under no such threat.

While this book is focused primarily on the adult use of marijuana, we would be remiss if we didn't mention the steps the government has taken to increase the spread of random student drug testing in private and public schools. In 2006 alone, the drug czar's office, in conjunction with the Department of Education, granted a total of approximately $8 million to sixty-six school districts in the United States to fund random student drug testing.[7] The Supreme Court lent its support to this effort in 2002 when it ruled that forcing students to undergo drug testing in order to participate in extracurricular activities did not violate the U.S. Constitution. Of course, we do not advocate the use of pot by adolescents. Still, common sense says that if teens believe they might get in trouble for using marijuana on the weekend, but will be safe—in terms of not being punished—if they indulge in alcohol, then they will most likely choose alcohol. For those who are truly concerned about the health of our nation's teens, this is hardly the optimal outcome.

Making an Example out of Athletes

In the sports world, the Michael Phelps controversy was anything but unusual. While his indulgence may have generated more head-lines than the actions of a lesser-known sport star would have, it was certainly not the first time a successful athlete had been raked over the coals for allegedly using marijuana. In fact, as we noted earlier, Phelps was not even the only athlete to generate pot-related headlines on Super Bowl Sunday 2009. Just four months prior to the big game, Pittsburgh Steelers wide receiver Santonio Holmes, who scored the game-winning touchdown and was named Most Valuable Player, had been deactivated by his team and fined $10,000 after he was arrested for having a small amount of marijuana in his car. In 2008, the National Football League (NFL) imposed a simi-lar one-game suspension on New England Patriots running back Kevin Faulk, who pled guilty to marijuana possession charges after an off-duty cop caught him with a few marijuana-filled cigars at a nightclub. He also lost two game checks as a result of his off-the-field indiscretion. In all, Faulk's financial punishment for this minor act of possession was approximately $300,000!

More famously, after failing repeated NFL-mandated drug tests for pot, Miami Dolphins all-pro running back Ricky Williams announced his decision to retire from football, albeit temporarily, rather than participate in a league that prohibited his off-field use of marijuana. (Williams stated that he used cannabis therapeutically to treat symptoms of social anxiety.) The star athlete faced a virtual nonstop torrent of public and media criticism for his decision. Of course, had he just gone along with the status quo and consumed alcohol when he wished to relax—like all of the "good" NFL players do—there would have been no disciplinary action, no media outcry, and no reason for the all-pro running back to have even considered retirement.

Brad Miller, at the time a center for the Sacramento Kings in the National Basketball Association, also discovered the detrimental consequences of using marijuana to relax. In 2008, the league suspended him for five games after he tested positive for marijuana for the third time. This suspension cost him $693,000 in lost salary. In an interview with the *Sacramento Bee* following the suspension, Miller explained that he smoked pot to alleviate stress and to help him get to sleep. "It obviously wasn't the right thing to do," he said, "but it was helpful to my mental state."[8] Miller further acknowledged that he had begun using marijuana more frequently after making the decision to reduce his consumption of alcohol.

Professional athletes, perhaps more than any other group of individuals, understand and appreciate the value of being in peak physical condition. Their livelihoods depend upon them performing to the absolute best of their abilities. If they believe that relaxing with cannabis is less detrimental to their bodies than drinking alcohol, then what logical reason do professional-sport leagues have for prohibiting this option? Perhaps athletic associations, and the public, will ponder this question in the future.

The Best Propaganda Money Can Buy

In chapter 5 we elaborated upon some of the popular myths and distortions promulgated by the federal government and by law enforcement to scare Americans into supporting marijuana prohibition. Whether it is the alleged gateway theory or claims regarding pot's supposed association with psychotic behavior, the collective impact of these falsehoods has been, and continues to be, highly damaging to marijuana-law-reform efforts.

In the mid-1990s, antimarijuana zealots in the U.S. government—led by a former army general—demanded even greater resources to assist in their efforts to lie to the public. Whereas in the past they had been firing shots across the bow, they decided it was time to load up and fire some cannons.

The turning point occurred in November 1996, when marijuana-law-reform advocates in California and Arizona sent shockwaves across the country by passing statewide voter initiatives in support of the medical use of cannabis. Although Arizona's law was later voided by the legislature, the voters had sent an unambiguous message: marijuana prohibition was losing popularity.

In Washington, D.C., it was clear to federal bureaucrats that the public no longer considered marijuana policy reform a fringe issue. Rather, it had demonstrated the potential to garner widespread voter support. And one could only assume, given the changing demographics of the country, that the public's support for more liberal marijuana laws would continue to grow. That is, unless the drug czar's office intervened.

Just nine days after the 1996 election, Clinton administration drug czar—retired general Barry McCaffrey—convened a meeting of about forty antidrug leaders in Washington. Invitees to the meeting included various staffers from the ONDCP and the DEA, as well as leaders from the Partnership for a Drug-Free America (PDFA), a nonprofit agency that had to that point coordinated the sole antidrug advertising campaign in the country (think, "This is your brain on drugs"). Participants openly discussed the political implications of the California and Arizona initiative results and attempted to develop a strategy to "stop the spread of legalization to [the] other 48 states."[9]

The general consensus of participants at the meeting was that they were being outspent by their opponents. This assumption was, quite ironically, inaccurate. Nevertheless, McCaffrey and others believed they needed money from the federal government to launch a mainstream media offensive to counter the messages of those who favored loosening America's marijuana laws. Former-PDFA president Richard Bonnette, according to notes from the meeting, stated the case clearly: "We lost Round I—no coordinated communication strategy. Didn't have media."[10] Another PDFA representative commented that initiating a high-profile media campaign would require an estimated $175 million—a total far larger than their organization possessed—and that they should ask for the federal government to pay for it.[11] Not surprisingly, members of Congress agreed.

McCaffrey and his brethren found that congressional leaders were eager to continue the culture war against marijuana users. In 1998, federal legislators enacted the Drug-Free Media Campaign Act, creating what would eventually become the National Youth Anti-Drug Media Campaign. Improving upon the initial $175 million annual funding request from PDFA, the Act authorized $195 million a year for five years. (Congress eventually provided the drug czar with $930 million of that potential $975 million amount.[12]) In the six years that followed, Congress allocated some $600 million more in funding. The vast majority of this money was used to produce and air public-service announcements demonizing marijuana use.

But the feds weren't always overt in their antimarijuana messaging. Far from it. During the height of the federal government's antipot advertising campaign, the drug czar's office engaged in a unique and insidious method of disseminating their propaganda—a method that was made possible because the original congressional legislation mandated television networks to sell ad time for antidrug ads at half their normal price. When the networks balked at this money-losing proposition, the drug czar's office proposed an ingenious alternative. The networks could receive "credit" if they incorporated antidrug messages into the scripts of popular television shows. The networks took the drug czar's office up on the offer— clandestinely incorporating government approved antipot themes on shows like *ER* and *Beverly Hills 90210*—and saved about $25 million in the process.[13] One participant in the scheme acknowledged, "Script changes would be discussed between ONDCP and the show—negotiated."[14] Fortunately, following the departure of General McCaffrey in 2001, the acting director of ONDCP, Ed Jurith, killed this quid-pro-quo arrangement.[15] Predictably, some members of Congress expressed dismay over the demise of this propaganda slush fund. Representative Elijah Cummings, who would later be terribly disappointed by Michael Phelps, admitted that he was "pretty comfortable" with the arrangement with the networks and found the change "upsetting." "I thought it was a creative way," he said, "to send a clear message."[16]

Eventually, several academic reviews of the drug czar's media campaign determined that it was *at best* ineffective. One study by researchers at Texas State University reported that the ad campaign was having a "boomerang effect" upon viewers, whereby the ads produced "a response that is precisely the opposite of what the ads' creators intended."[17] In other words, the campaign was actually *encouraging* marijuana use by young people. In fact, the more often teens viewed the government's ads, the more likely they were to want to try pot!

Ultimately, most members of Congress recognized the National Youth Anti-Drug Media Campaign was, pardon the pun, a bust. While they have not yet eliminated the program altogether, they have quietly and steadily reduced appropriations for the advertising campaign from $180 million for the 2001 fiscal year to $60 million for 2008.[18] But the media campaign certainly had enjoyed a good run. Whether or not it had any beneficial impact on reducing teen marijuana use, the more than $1.5 *billion* spent between 1998 and 2008 undoubtedly contributed to the antimarijuana bias that exists in our society.

The Role of the Media in Maintaining Prohibition

The worldwide media frenzy over Michael Phelps's alleged toke illustrates the power the media wields in advancing the federal government's antimarijuana agenda. Phelps's infamous bong hit never would have been a matter of public record had the international media outlet, Great Britain's *News of the World*, not published the photo. Yet once they did, news bureaus around the globe jumped on the story as if Phelps had been caught socializing with Osama Bin Laden. And while a broad range of commentators eventually decried the media's overreaction (and many pundits even defended Phelps's token toke), the majority of news reports clearly conveyed the impression that Phelps had done something morally wrong and that he deserved to be punished.

Of course, all of you who read chapter 4 know that the media's complicity in initiating and maintaining cannabis prohibition is hardly a new development. The mainstream media not only dutifully reports on marijuana escapades of the rich and famous, but it also helps to advance the antimarijuana agenda of the federal government. Over the decades, most media outlets have served the role of megaphone for the government's antipot crusade, generally echoing—rather than challenging—the feds' outrageous and typically unsubstantiated reefer rhetoric. Sometimes the government and the fourth estate have even worked together hand in hand. For instance, in 1997 the National Association of Broadcasters announced that it was joining forces with the government and the Partnership for a Drug Free America to "join the fight against drug abuse."[19] The following year, the Magazine Publishers of America proclaimed that it would collaborate with and provide "editorial support" for the Clinton administration's antimarijuana efforts.[20]

More recently, and perhaps most alarmingly, in 2005, the Government Accountability Office (GAO) determined that the Office of National Drug Control Policy had violated a federal ban on, appropriately enough, "covert propaganda" by using National Youth Anti-Drug Media Campaign funds to produce and distribute "video news releases" for local television stations to air on their nightly news broadcasts.[21] The videos, which were distributed to approximately 770 news stations nationwide between the years

2002 and 2004, were designed "to be indistinguishable from news stories produced by private sector television news organizations," the GAO found. "ONDCP did this so they could be seamlessly incorporated into private sector television news broadcasts without alteration," the GAO continued, making it "impossible for the targeted viewing audience to ascertain that these stories were produced by the government, and not by the news organization broadcasting them." Following the GAO determination, the practice ended, but not before these "reports" had aired in more than 22 million homes![22]

Follow the Money

All of the factors above contribute to an atmosphere whereby tens of millions of Americans naturally shy away from the use of marijuana, primarily out of fear of punishment. That point is indisputable.

Further, we contend that this artificial reduction in marijuana use leads to the greater use of alcohol among the public. If you consider the total number of Americans consuming alcohol every week, common sense dictates that at least some of them—or perhaps many of them—would occasionally or regularly use marijuana instead if there were absolutely no sanctions or stigma associated with its use.

What is debatable, however, is whether elected officials, corporate leaders, and regulatory bodies like USA Swimming are sincere in their efforts to try to reduce marijuana use, or are they *intentionally* driving people to drink? As we consider the motivations of these entities' actions, we would like to remind you of the old adage: Follow the money.

Let's take the athletic institutions first, specifically those involved in the suspensions of Michael Phelps and Ricky Williams. Surely USA Swimming, recognized by the U.S. Olympic Committee as the national governing body for the sport of swimming, did not suspend the 2008 USOC Sportsman of the Year without consulting with the Olympic Committee first. When confronted with the news that Phelps had been drinking excessively and smoking a little pot, might the USOC have perceived any conflict of interest knowing that Anheuser-Busch, maker of Budweiser beer, was the official "international beer sponsor" for the 2008 Olympics and that its brands are the "official beer" of the USOC itself? The financial terms of this arrangement are not public, but securing the use of the Olympic logo for use on products in thirty countries around the world can hardly come cheap. Similarly, when deciding whether to sanction players like Ricky Williams or Kevin Faulk, how heavily does it weigh in the mind of NFL executives that the league and its respective teams annually receive more than $100 million combined from sponsorship deals with beer makers like Coors and Anheuser-Busch? If there is one thing sports executives understand it is competition, and there is no doubt that marijuana and beer are competing products. Is it plausible that the enemy of their friend has become *their* enemy?

As far as America's elected officials go, it would be nice to believe that their actions, however misguided, were based on genuine concerns regarding the public's use of pot. In some cases, they may be. But when pondering politicians' antimarijuana motives, it is difficult to ignore the presence of a powerful Washington, D.C., lobby: the National Beer Wholesalers Association.

Interestingly, the National Beer Wholesalers Association started flexing its financial muscles on Capitol Hill to a far greater degree around the same time that Congress and the drug czar's office launched the National Youth Anti-Drug Media Campaign. In the 1997–98 political cycle, the NBWA contributed just $1.3 million to federal candidates. In the 1999–2000 and 2001–2 cycles, their contributions jumped to $1.87 million and $2.07 million, respectively, placing them in the top twelve among all political action committees (PACs). But America's beer lobby was just getting warmed up. In the three political cycles between 2003 and 2008 combined, the NBWA gave more than $8 million to federal candidates and ranked among the top five most generous PACs each cycle, reaching the no. 2 slot in 2005–6.[23]

What did the NBWA buy with this money? It's hard to say. But consider this: The use of alcohol is illegal for teens, and a strong case can be made (as we are doing with this book) that it is far more harmful for the user than marijuana. Yet the original bill authorizing the Media Campaign specifically *banned* the use of campaign funds to address underage drinking. In fact, when lawmakers attempt to amend the bill so that anti-alcohol messages could be included, the NBWA strongly opposed the amendment.[24] To this day, the National Youth Anti-Drug Media Campaign has remained almost entirely alcohol-free. Conversely, when congressional leaders reauthorized the Media Campaign in 2006, they inserted a provision encouraging the drug czar to keep positioning marijuana as Public Enemy No. 1. The provision reads, "In conducting advertising and activities otherwise authorized under this section, the Director may emphasize prevention of youth marijuana use."[25]

With respect to America's criminal policies, it also appears that the alcohol industry plays a role in the maintenance of prohibition. This was most certainly the case in 2008 when the California Beer and Beverage Distributors contributed $100,000 to the campaign against Proposition 5, the Nonviolent Offender Rehabilitation Act (NORA).[26] This initiative proposed to, among other things, reduce the penalty for cannabis possession in California from a misdemeanor to an infraction, similar to a traffic ticket. This change would have ensured that those caught with marijuana would not be burdened with criminal records for the rest of their lives. Why did the beverage industry oppose Proposition 5? One can only speculate, but it seems likely that this was a good old-fashioned turf battle. The proposed reductions in marijuana penalties were a direct threat to their business.

In the end, despite the evidence presented, we can't say for certain whether all of the entities described in this chapter are intentionally driving Americans toward alcohol through their antimarijuana actions. Regardless of their motivations, however, the bottom line is that their collective efforts are contributing to a definite outcome: less marijuana use and more alcohol use. Tragically, this result is leading, as we will see in the following chapter, to a shocking array of damaging effects upon our society.

chapter seven

The Real-World Ramifications of Our Pro-Alcohol Culture

Virtually every sexual assault is associated with alcohol abuse.
Almost every assault of any kind is related to drinking.
—C. D. "Dan" Mote, president,
University of Maryland, August 2008[1]

Given the widespread popularity of both marijuana and alcohol as social and recreational intoxicants, it's hardly surprising to discover that the two substances are potential substitutes for one another. Yet, as we explained in chapter 6, our society steers citizens who might otherwise enjoy relaxing with cannabis toward the use of alcohol instead. In other words, by artificially reducing the use of marijuana in this country, we are artificially increasing the level of alcohol use—and all of the problems that go along with that use.

So what are some of the real-world ramifications of this practice? To begin our assessment, it seems only appropriate that we look to MTV's long-running reality show *The Real World*, which since 1992 has purported to demonstrate what happens when young Americans "stop being polite and start getting real." Yet there is something decidedly unreal about the social lives of the show's cast members. In more than twenty seasons, including more than 140 cast members representing the eighteen-to-twenty-nine-year-old demographic, viewers have never once witnessed anyone chilling on the couch after taking a hit off a joint or a bong.

Instead, season after season, cast members—including the under-twenty-one housemates—drink to their hearts' content. Viewers have seen drunken young women performing in public like strippers and they have witnessed inebriated male and female cast members engaging in random sexual hookups. Excessive drinking on the set has frequently led to heated arguments among castmates, fights, abusive language, and overly aggressive actions toward women. In some cases, these actions have even led to arrests. Hangovers and blackouts on *The Real World* are just a fact of life. Yet despite all of this alcohol-fueled debauchery, there is no indication that the show's producers have ever considered taking steps to reduce cast members' alcohol intake—even though two housemates ultimately entered rehab for alcoholism during the filming of the show. If anything, it seems as if the prevalence of alcohol-fueled episodes on the show have increased over time—as has the proliferation of alcohol-inducing play things like pool tables and hot tubs—to the point where one could only assume that producers are encouraging the use of booze. This was undoubtedly the case when they arranged for the suitemates in *The Real World: Las Vegas* to work for a nightclub and even serve cocktails.

Is the real world exactly like *The Real World*? Well, no. First of all, surveys indicate that residents of the real world often use marijuana and typically have ready access to it. In addition, most people have actual responsibilities that diminish their ability to get shit-faced six or seven nights a week. These two points aside, however, the comparison is spot-on.

We live in a society that has created something of an intoxication-related balloon effect. The balloon effect describes a situation where the proactive prohibition of one action produces a similar counter-action—like when you squeeze one end of a balloon, you simply shift air to the other end. This analogy is often applied to efforts to eradicate illegal drug crops in South America or Afghanistan. For instance, if authorities exert pressure to try to eliminate the cultivation of coca crops in Columbia, production will simply increase in Peru or some other nation. In the real world, like on *The Real World*, we exist within a society where pressure is being applied to the marijuana end of the balloon. As a result, air is shifted to the alcohol end, and its use has expanded. Let's take a look at what this expansion has wrought.

Campus Life

Before we touch upon the university policies that steer students toward alcohol (or fail to counter societal pressures to drink) and the unfortunate impact of these policies, it is worth considering for a moment the fact that students are, in many ways, conditioned for an alcohol-based campus culture before they even matriculate. George W. Dowdall discusses this predisposition in his book *College Drinking: Reframing a Social Problem*.

> While it has become fashionable in some quarters to talk about college heavy drinking as an epidemic, it is one that many students freely choose. But what they want is shaped powerfully in popular culture, much of it skillfully manipulated by the advertising of the alcohol industry. A significant core of college drinkers come to college not only expecting but also seeking a party-centered lifestyle, and colleges hardly stand in their way.[2]

Campuses are a microcosm of the broader society when it comes to alcohol and marijuana use. Although both substances are illegal for students under the age of twenty-one, the punishments for those who use them are far from equal. Most universities impose policies mandating that students who are busted using cannabis will face more severe sanctions than students caught drinking alcohol. We are aware of numerous students who have been removed from campus housing for possessing a small amount of marijuana in their dorm room. Yet these same students would have received a slap on the wrist—most likely in the form of a warning or campus probation—if alcohol had been present.

Take Purdue University in Indiana, for example. This school imposes a "zero tolerance" policy for students who are caught with marijuana in their dorms. This means that the possession of any amount of cannabis will result in immediate cancellation of their campus housing contract. By contrast, Purdue employs a "three strikes" policy for underage possession of alcohol. Bob Heitert, director of administration for university residence halls at Purdue, justifies the school's inconsistent policy this way: "Illegal drugs are against the law for everyone, while alcohol is against the law for a larger portion of students but not for everyone. Society seems to take a different approach to alcohol than they do to illegal drugs. We reflect that societal difference."[3]

Of course, universities like Purdue are under no obligation to kick students out of campus housing for minor marijuana offenses. In fact, in many places this campus-imposed penalty is far more severe than any sanctions a student would face for violating their *state* marijuana laws, which typically punish first-time offenders with a fine or probation.

Sure, we acknowledge that university governments are bound by a responsibility to punish behavior that is not consistent with the law. But they are not legally obligated to establish stringent penalties, such as enforcing zero-tolerance housing policies or barring students with minor pot violations from ever holding student office, as is the policy of the University of Maryland at College Park.[4] More importantly, they are under no legal obligation to treat students who illegally possess marijuana on campus more severely than they sanction students who illegally possess alcohol. Yet most colleges do—and often for no reason other than a perceived need to reflect existing societal differences. And by maintaining these policies in the face of student opposition (a subject we touch upon in chapter 10), university governments and their boards of trustees are making a conscious, if inadvertent, decision to steer students toward the use of alcohol.

And what are the ramifications of these kinds of campus policies? Like on *The Real World*, the picture isn't pretty. First, the use of alcohol by college students is rampant. According to data from the Harvard School of Public Health College Alcohol Study, approximately 80 percent of college students drink alcohol.[5] Figures for binge drinking are even more startling. For instance, more than 44 percent of students surveyed in 2001 said that they had engaged in binge drinking in the preceding two weeks, and more than 22 percent had done so at least three times in that time period.[6] Predictably, these frequent binge drinkers—and those around them—often suffer as a result. As described by Dowdall in *College Drinking,* "[F]requent binge drinkers were 7 to 10 times more likely than the nonbinge drinkers to get into trouble with the campus police, damage property or get injured, not use protection when having sex, or engage in unplanned sexual activity."[7]

The social consequences of all of this student drinking are even more alarming. At the most tragic level, alcohol abuse is a leading cause of fatalities on college campuses. In 2001, there were an estimated 1,700 alcohol-related unintentional-injury deaths among college students and others aged 18 to 24.[8] These deaths are just the tip of the alcohol-related-injury iceberg. Researchers estimate that every year approximately 600,000 students between the ages of 18 and 24 are unintentionally injured while under the influence of alcohol.[9] Of course, those who drink are not the only ones adversely affected. Even more disturbing is the number of injuries to others that are caused by students under the influence of alcohol. It is estimated that each year approximately 700,000 students between the ages of 18 and 24 are assaulted by students who have been drinking, and close to 100,000 students between the ages of 18 and 24 are victims of alcohol-related sexual assault or date rape.[10] Yet these raw numbers only tell part of the story. The much broader impact of alcohol abuse on campus is evident when one looks at the percentage of violent acts that are booze-related. According to a 1994 report by the National Center on Addiction and Substance Abuse (CASA), 95 percent of all campus assaults are alcohol-related, and 90 percent of all reported campus rapes involve a victim or an assailant who has been drinking alcohol.[11]

University officials are well aware of these startling statistics. As is evident by the quote at the beginning of this chapter, campus leaders not only recognize that alcohol is a frequent cause of injuries and assaults, but many also believe that it is a factor in almost *all* campus assaults. Think about this point for a moment. These same officials are aware that students use marijuana on their campuses—most likely to a greater extent than they would like. Yet despite pot's popularity among the student body, you rarely if ever hear university officials or campus police publicly blaming assaults or rapes on marijuana abuse. In other words, the people responsible for maintaining safety on college campuses recognize that alcohol use frequently leads to widespread injuries and violent student behavior while marijuana use does not. You would think that leaders of institutions of higher learning would rationally and impartially examine this data and act accordingly. Think again.

Confronted with this nationwide college-drinking epidemic, university leaders have generally concluded that the best approach to this problem is to instruct students, including underage students, how to consume booze more responsibly. In short, universities are implicitly, and in some cases explicitly, endorsing alcohol as the only acceptable recreational substance of choice for students.

So how are universities attempting to encourage students to moderate their intake of alcohol? One popular method is to promote "social norms," meaning that university officials educate young people about other students' drinking habits (which tend to be lower than otherwise assumed) as well as their attitudes toward abusive drinking by others. The belief behind this strategy is that students will learn to appreciate that they do not need to drink to excess to fit in with one another, and will recognize that many of their peers find overindulgence in alcohol to be a turnoff. These are laudable goals, of course. Yet the schizophrenic nature of this pro-alcohol/ anti-alcohol campaign is all too apparent. Take the e-CHUG program, for example.[12] This program is widely used by universities across the country and is sometimes even a requirement for first-year students. While its purpose is to show students, through the use of personal surveys, the potentially problematic and atypical nature of their drinking, the name of the program sends just the opposite message to participants. Welcome to college everyone! Here's a nice "CHUG" email to set the tone for the next four (or more) years! Now drink responsibly—and don't "chug" too much!

Similarly, in the introduction of this book we described a prominent effort among university presidents to address the problem of alcohol abuse and related violence on campuses. The more than 130 members of the Amethyst Initiative have publicly called for a national debate on lowering the drinking age to eighteen years of age. Proponents of this measure believe that this change will bring student drinking out into the open and will lead to more responsible behavior.

However one feels about the merits of this proposal, there is no arguing that it is based on the assumption that college students are going to drink alcohol one way or the other, and that the best outcome our society can hope for is some kind of moderation of this behavior. But we contend that this assessment is incomplete and pose an alternative question. That is: If both alcohol and marijuana are currently illegal for those under the age of twenty-one, why is it acceptable to encourage college students to "drink responsibly," but not appropriate to suggest that they should "party responsibly" with marijuana instead? More specifically, if 130 university presidents believe we should have a debate about making alcohol legal for students under twenty-one, shouldn't they also endorse a similar discussion regarding whether to make a less harmful substance available as a legal alternative?

Societal Costs

Of course college students are not the only Americans negatively affected by society's excessive use of alcohol. These days alcohol abuse is widespread, and its negative effects on the health and safety of our populace is staggering. The public's use of booze imposes massive personal and financial burdens. From lost productivity to hospitalizations to criminal justice expenditures, alcohol use and abuse costs this nation close to $200 *billion* annually—and perhaps more. The most frequently cited figures estimating the overall cost of alcohol abuse in this country come from a pair of National Institute on Alcohol Abuse and Alcoholism reports entitled *Economic Costs of Alcohol Abuse in the United States*, published in 1992 and in 1998. Unfortunately, these reports were not updated during the entire tenure of the George W. Bush administration—perhaps because they were spending all of their antidrug funding on producing antimarijuana ads—so we can only assume, based on the approximately 25 percent increase in overall costs from 1992 ($148 billion) to 1998 ($184.6 billion), that today's alcohol-related costs are well above the 1998 total.

Regardless of whether the current annual cost of alcohol use in our society is $150 billion, $185 billion, or somewhere over $200 billion, these reports indicate that there are a variety of factors contributing to this gargantuan total. The most significant factor is "lost productivity due to alcohol-related illness." The *Economic Costs* reports provide the following explanation of how this figure was achieved: "[Determining lost productivity due to alcohol or drug dependence] involves comparing the expected value of earnings for an individual who is alcohol or drug dependent with his or her expected earnings in the absence of the alcohol or drug disorder. The difference between these two values is the estimated impact of the disorder on the individual, and the sum of these estimated impacts across all individuals with alcohol or drug disorders is the estimated national total impact."[13] In 1998, researchers estimated that alcohol-related productivity loss imposed an estimated financial toll on the nation of more than $86 billion.[14]

Similarly, these studies also measured lost productivity for persons incarcerated for alcohol-related crimes, a factor that cost more than $9 billion in 1998. On top of these totals, researchers included additional costs associated with the medical consequences of alcohol consumption—essentially health care costs—which totaled more than $15 billion in 1998. Another $36.5 billion was attributable to lost future earnings because of premature deaths, $8.6 billion of which were due to deaths in alcohol-related motor vehicle accidents. (Worldwide, alcohol is estimated to be responsible for 4 percent of all premature deaths![15])

Alcohol-related crime also imposes significant costs upon society. A study by the U.S. Department of Justice's Office of Juvenile Justice and Delinquency Prevention estimated the cost of alcohol-attributable violent crime by juveniles (defined as those under age twenty-one) at nearly $30 billion in 1996. More than three-quarters of this total was attributable to the victims' pain and lost quality of life. Direct medical costs were responsible for another $1.1 billion.[16] Certainly this figure would be significantly higher if it included violent crimes committed by individuals of all ages.

Of course, what makes these figures all the more problematic is that our government drives people toward the use of alcohol and away from cannabis, despite indisputable evidence that marijuana would impose fewer costs on society. Let's start with the approximately $28 billion in future earnings lost because of premature deaths due to alcohol (not including motor vehicle accidents). Since marijuana is not adversely associated with mortality, we could theoretically reduce this number if adults were allowed—or perhaps even encouraged—to use marijuana instead of alcohol. Similarly, marijuana use is not associated with an increased likelihood of violent behavior, so we could expect that a shift from the use of alcohol to marijuana would potentially lead to a reduction in alcohol-related violent crime as well.

With respect to medical costs, marijuana's impact is extremely limited compared to alcohol. While it is difficult to find studies comparing the direct health care costs attributable to booze and pot in the United States, one study in Canada—where marijuana is used at rates comparable to those in America—determined that annual alcohol-related health care costs were *forty-five times greater* than marijuana-related health care costs! According to the study, in 2002 health care costs stemming from the use of alcohol totaled $3.3 billion, compared to just $73 million from marijuana.[17]

With respect to lost productivity attributable to marijuana use, it is difficult to find a figure to compare to the $86-billion price tag attributed to "alcohol-related illness." That is because the description of "drug dependence" used by the federal government to calculate the figure for productivity lost due to drug-related illness (which was estimated at $23 billion in 1998) is defined as whether an individual had used marijuana *or cocaine* more than 100 times in his lifetime.[18] In other words, despite the federal government's vigorous antimarijuana efforts between 1998 and 2008, drug czars McCaffrey and Walters somehow never managed to produce a study showing that marijuana use alone has a significant impact on the public's productivity. In fact, when Walters's ONDCP published a booklet entitled "Marijuana Myths & Facts: The Truth Behind 10 Popular Misconceptions," with twenty-two pages of text loaded with eighty-three footnotes, it included just one minor reference to productivity: "Marijuana also harms society by causing lost productivity in business." Interestingly, the drug czar's office provided no reference to affirm this allegation.

Beyond the pure financial burden to society, alcohol, in some situations, can also have a negative impact on the public's quality of life. Here we are not referring to hangovers or to family discord, but the personal discomfort that is often caused by the drinking of others. For example, there have been many articles written in recent years about the problems stemming from overindulgence in alcohol prior to and during sporting events. In one instance in 2004, a fan and his nine-year-old son were repeatedly harassed during a Colorado Rockies game by drunken fans who intentionally spilled beer on them. When this same fan filed a lawsuit against the Rockies for failing to discourage excessive drinking at the stadium, the team flippantly replied in its filing, "The possibility that beer might be spilled by spectators in large sporting events is [an] inherent risk."[19] The National Football League, on the other hand, appears to fully recognize the problem of fan drunkenness and is taking it far more seriously. Consider this excerpt from a 2008 *Washington Post* article: "At the behest of Commissioner Roger Goodell, all 32 teams have announced a fan conduct policy in an attempt to make their stadiums more fan-friendly. Goodell said he believes fans should be able to watch without being subjected to abusive language, obscene gestures and other forms of rude behavior."[20] In fact, in order to curb such rowdy behavior, some NFL teams have even gone so far as to ban alcohol sales during games.

Of course, by emphasizing these negative behaviors we are not dismissing the fact that booze, particularly when consumed in moderation, also frequently serves to improve one's quality of life—whether it is wine at a dinner party or cocktails at happy hour. Rather, we are simply acknowledging that alcohol is also routinely associated with unpleasant behaviors in a manner that marijuana use is not.

Alcohol and Violence

"[I]f you talk to a policeman on a beat in any one of these American cities, alcohol is a mildly addictive, readily available drug that is responsible for more damage in our society than any other drug on the street. And it is also associated in a dramatic way with violent behavior."[21]
—BARRY MCCAFFREY, FORMER U.S. DRUG CZAR, 1998

In the "Campus Life" section, we detailed numerous ways that alcohol contributes to violent and aggressive behavior at colleges and universities. Of course, alcohol-related violence is not limited just to institutions of higher learning; it is rampant throughout our society. In fact, the extent to which alcohol is associated with violent crime is arguably far greater than the average person appreciates. The following excerpt from the federal government's report, *The Economic Costs of Alcohol and Drug Abuse in the United States 1992*, provides an overview of the problem:

> Numerous studies have found that problem drinkers, alcohol abusers, and alcoholics appear to be over-represented among adults convicted of violent crimes, and people convicted of violent crime often report alcohol consumption immediately prior to their crime. Furthermore, research demonstrates that the degree of aggressive response is proportional to the amount of alcohol consumed. Empirical data on jail and prison inmates suggest that alcohol consumption also appears to be associated with violence. Inmates are more likely to have been under the influence of alcohol prior to a violent crime than for an economic crime or other types of crime.[22]

So what are the raw figures? The U.S. government estimates that alcohol contributes to 25 to 30 percent of all violent crime in the America, including 30 percent of homicides and 22.5 percent of sexual assaults. However, the approach federal researchers used to calculate these figures attributes the use of alcohol as a primary cause of violent behavior in *only 50 percent of the cases* where the perpetrator had been drinking.[23] Yes, you read that correctly. In order to be conservative with their estimates, researchers only consider booze to be a contributing factor in half of the cases in which alcohol was actually involved. This means that in reality alcohol was involved in some manner in 60 percent of homicides and almost half of all sexual assaults. Regardless of whether the estimates are conservative or not, the raw figures are striking. According to federal government data, 7,655 homicides in the Unites States in 2001 were attributable to excessive alcohol use.[24] Alcohol use is also frequently associated with domestic and partner violence. According to a 2002 report by the U.S. Department of Justice, two-thirds of victims who suffered violence by a partner reported that alcohol played a role, and among spouse victims, three out of four reported that the offender had been drinking.[25]

Of course, alcohol-related violence is not limited solely to the United States. Similar trends exist throughout the world. A 2006 World Health Organization report assessing alcohol use and violence included the following statistics:

- In England and Wales, 50% of victims of interpersonal violence reported that the perpetrator was under the influence of alcohol at the time of assault.
- In Russia, around three-quarters of individuals arrested for homicide had consumed alcohol shortly before the incident.
- In South Africa, 44% of victims of interpersonal violence believed that their attacker was under the influence of alcohol.
- In Tianjin, China, a study of inmates found that 50% of defendants convicted of assault had been drinking alcohol prior to the incident.[26]

We recognize that alcohol's association with violence remains a controversial subject in some circles. Some experts, especially those in the domestic violence community, argue that violence is not caused by alcohol per se; rather, they assert that abusive partners possess personality traits that contribute to both their drinking and their violent behavior. We are sympathetic to this viewpoint and do not wish to create the impression that alcohol is the sole cause of domestic violence. That said, most domestic violence experts acknowledge that booze is a serious risk factor in abusive relationships. For example, a team of investigators at the University of Buffalo assessed the impact of alcohol use in relationships with histories of interpersonal violence. They concluded that incidents of male-to-female physical aggression were eight times more likely on days when men drank as compared to days when they did not. Acts of *severe* male-to-female physical aggression were eleven times more likely on days when men consumed alcohol.[27] In a follow-up study examining the effects of alcohol and other psychoactive drugs— cannabis, cocaine, and heroin—on interpersonal violence, investigators again found that alcohol significantly increased the likelihood of male partner violence (as did cocaine). Conversely, cannabis was not associated with an increased likelihood of physical aggression.[28]

Of course, the use of alcohol alone does not always instigate violent behavior, but as the University of Buffalo researchers found, this behavior is far more likely to occur on nights when drinking takes place. So when we propose that legalizing marijuana would likely lead to a reduction in domestic and community violence, we are envisioning a future where marijuana is not only legal, but where domestic violence counselors feel it is appropriate to advise abusive partners to reduce or eliminate their alcohol intake by consuming marijuana as an alternative.

As we noted in the previous chapter, in the professional sports world, league officials have taken the exact opposite approach. By default, pro athletes generally do not have the option to consume any recreational intoxicant other than alcohol. As a result, they often find themselves in bars or at nightclubs where alcohol and violence regularly mix. National Basketball Association star Paul Pierce was in a nightclub in 2000 when he was stabbed eleven times. NFL star Plaxico Burress was in a nightclub in 2008 when he accidentally shot himself in the leg with a gun he carried for his own protection. And NFL star Adam "Pac Man" Jones was in a nightclub in 2007 when he was involved in a shooting that left a bouncer at the club paralyzed. As these types of events have become more frequent, it's hardly any wonder that former NFL star Chris Carter told ESPN, "The number one problem in the NFL isn't steroids, it's alcohol."[29]

From Bud(weiser) to Bud?

Would legalizing marijuana eliminate all of these problems? Of course not. But returning to the balloon analogy we described at the beginning of this chapter, what would happen if we took some pressure off the marijuana end of the balloon by amending our pot laws? Or what if we were even more aggressive and applied some pressure on the alcohol end of the balloon by encouraging people to reduce their alcohol intake by using marijuana instead? This scenario may almost be too much for even some supportive readers of this book to imagine at this time, but it is a situation certainly worth pondering—especially when we consider the kind of behavior our society is encouraging today.

PART THREE

Freedom of Choice

chapter eight

You Would Think This Would Be Enough: Traditional Arguments Against Marijuana Prohibition

Beginning in the late 1960s, a handful of loosely organized advocacy groups began to publicly advance the cause of reforming America's criminal marijuana laws. The most prominent of these groups was NORML—the National Organization for the Reform of Marijuana Laws—which formed in 1970.

NORML, along with a small coalition of doctors and lawyers, started lobbying state politicians and the public regarding the need to cease arresting adults who were using marijuana responsibly in the privacy of their own home. NORML's arguments, which typically hinged on the notion that America's overly punitive pot policies were more detrimental to both the user and to society than was the use of marijuana itself, were persuasive in convincing states to make incremental changes to their marijuana prohibition laws.

Between 1970 and 1979, most state legislatures reduced their marijuana possession penalties from felonies to misdemeanors. Eleven states took steps to "decriminalize" minor marijuana-possession offenses, a policy that was initially recommended by the National Commission on Marihuana and Drug Abuse in 1972.[1]

Under these laws, states replaced criminal penalties for minor pot offenses with fine-only sanctions and removed the possibility that offenders would be sentenced to prison.

Yet by the 1980s, public and political opinion became less tolerant of liberalizing America's marijuana laws. So-called parents groups, led predominantly by suburban mothers warning of the dangers (both real and, more often than not, imaginary) pot posed to children, began dominating the public and political discourse. As a result, state and federal politicians ceased entertaining efforts to reduce marijuana penalties, and public support for cannabis legalization dwindled to less than 20 percent.

However, by the mid-1990s several new nonprofit organizations—such as the Marijuana Policy Project and the Drug Policy Alliance—arrived on the scene to assist NORML with its multi-decade reform efforts. All of these organizations seek to advance their cause by highlighting the futility of prohibition, and by emphasizing the multitude of adverse and unintended consequences that this policy imposes upon the general public. In short, reformers maintain that modern marijuana prohibition is a "cure" that is far worse than the disease.

As in the 1970s, this line of argument has again proven effective at influencing politicians to undertake incremental reforms. Since 1996, more than a dozen states have enacted legal exemptions to allow for qualified patients to use cannabis, and two additional states have decriminalized the drug's use for all adults. Even more importantly, nationwide public support for legalizing the sale and use of marijuana by those aged twenty-one or older has steadily risen over the past two decades to over 40 percent. In fact, polling data released in early 2009 showed that a far greater percentage of Americans endorsed legalizing pot than supported the Republican Party.[2] Obviously, public opinion is heading in the right direction—even if overall support remains shy of a solid majority.

So let's explore some of most common and intellectually compelling arguments advanced by reform organizations in support of ending cannabis prohibition. In the remainder of this chapter, we'll focus on seven of these arguments.

1. Taxing and regulating marijuana would produce significant economic revenues for the federal and state governments.

Stop us if you've heard this one before: "Legalizing and taxing pot would wipe out the national debt." Well not exactly, but it would certainly help matters. According to a 2007 economic analysis by George Mason University professor Jon Gettman, the retail value of the U.S. marijuana market now stands at a whopping $113 billion per year. Using standard tax percentages obtained from the Office of Management and Budget, Gettman calculates that the diversion of $113 billion from the taxable economy into the illicit economy deprives taxpayers of $31.1 billion annually."[3]

In California alone, legalizing pot would potentially raise nearly $1.4 billion in annual tax revenue via excise taxes on cannabis production and sales taxes on consumer purchases, according to 2009 estimates by the California State Board of Equalization and Taxation.[4] A 2009 California NORML economic analysis called this figure overly conservative, noting that the agency failed to calculate the additional tax revenue that will be generated by the thousands of cannabis-related jobs and industries that likely will be created once pot is fully legalized.

"A legal market would generate additional benefits in the form of tourism and spin-off industries, such as coffee shops, paraphernalia, and industrial hemp," the report determined. "A comparable example would be California's wine industry. With $12.3 billion in retail sales, the wine industry generates 309,000 jobs, $10.1 billion in wages, and $2 billion in tourist expenditures. Extrapolating these figures to a legal marijuana market, . . . one might expect $12 to $18 billion in total economic activity, with 60,000 to 110,000 new jobs created, and $2.5 to $3.5 billion in legal wages, which would generate additional income and business taxes for the state."[5]

2. **Arresting more than 850,000 Americans each year for marijuana-related offenses is a waste of law enforcement resources, and is terribly destructive to the lives of otherwise law-abiding citizens.**

This argument tends to be the number one talking point among marijuana-law-reform advocates, and it is with good reason. Law enforcement agents have made over 20 million pot-related arrests since 1965, and the annual number of pot arrests is rising. In 2007, police made a record 873,000 marijuana arrests—9 out of 10 of which were for pot possession only, not marijuana cultivation or sale.[6] If current arrest trends continue, police will begin making over 1,000,000 pot-related busts per year by 2010.

These prosecutions come at a significant cost to taxpayers. A 2005 report by visiting Harvard economics professor Jeffrey Miron calculated that state and federal governments spend nearly $8 billion dollars per year to arrest, prosecute, and jail marijuana offenders.[7] Other analyses place this total at upwards of $10 billion per year.[8]

These prosecutions bring tremendous fiscal, professional, and emotional hardships upon those arrested. Pot-related run-ins with law enforcement carry a variety of severe penalties. As noted in chapter 6, these sanctions include probation and mandatory drug testing; loss of employment; loss of child custody; removal from subsidized housing; loss of student aid; loss of voting privileges; loss of adoption rights; and loss of certain federal welfare benefits, such as food stamps.

But that's not all. Tens of thousands of Americans are also serving prison time for pot. Nearly 13 percent of state inmates and just over 12 percent of federal inmates are incarcerated for marijuana-related drug violations, according to a 2006 Bureau of Justice Statistics report.[9] (The report did not include the estimated percentage of inmates incarcerated in county jails for pot-related offenses.)

In human terms, this means that some 34,000 state inmates and an estimated 11,000 federal inmates are serving time behind bars for violating marijuana laws. In fiscal terms, this means U.S. taxpayers are spending more than $1 billion annually just to imprison pot offenders.[10]

3. Enforcing marijuana laws limits law enforcement's capacity to address other, more serious crimes.

Law-enforcement resource allocation is a zero-sum gain. Every hour—or to be more accurate, hours[11]—police officers spend arresting and processing minor marijuana offenders is time they are *not* out on the streets protecting the public from more significant criminal activity. For example, at the same time marijuana arrests climbed dramatically in the 1990s, criminal arrests for cocaine and heroin declined sharply—implying that the increased enforcement of marijuana laws was achieved at the expense of enforcing laws against the possession and trafficking of more dangerous substances.[12] In New York City, pot arrests skyrocketed during the 1990s, from under 2,500 per year in 1992 to over 50,000 in the year 2000.[13] Not surprisingly, in the wake of the tragic terrorist attacks of September 11, police were instructed to turn their attention to other more serious criminal activities, and pot arrests fell sharply.

One notable study by Florida State University economists Bruce Benson and David Rasmussen determined that serious crimes, such as robbery and assault, increase proportionally when police focus their attention on drug law enforcement, particularly marijuana prohibition. Analyzing Florida state crime statistics, they reported that every 1 percent increase in drug arrests leads to a 0.18 percent increase in serious crimes.[14]

In short, directing police resources toward marijuana-law enforcement inevitably decreases resources that would have otherwise been dedicated to combating other crimes. Legalizing marijuana would allow law enforcement, prosecutors, and the courts to reallocate their existing resources toward activities that will more effectively target serious criminal behavior and keep the public safe.

4. The enforcement of marijuana laws is racially discriminatory and also disproportionately affects young adults.

Want to know prohibition's dirty little secret? It's this: Criminal marijuana-law enforcement disproportionately affects citizens by race and by age.

An analysis of marijuana-arrest data commissioned by NORML in 2000 found that African Americans are far more likely to be busted for pot possession than their white counterparts. "The black arrest rate for marijuana possession is greater than the white rate in 90 percent of the (700 metropolitan area) counties reviewed, and more than twice the white rate in 64 percent of them," the study concluded. "Racial differences in marijuana and other drug arrest rates are stark, unambiguous, and represent a serious threat to the integrity of our criminal justice system."[15]

A follow-up report commissioned by NORML in 2005 further highlighted this racial disparity. It found that adult African Americans accounted for only 12 percent of annual marijuana users, but made up 23 percent of all marijuana possession arrests in the United States.[16]

A 2008 ACLU investigation of marijuana arrests in New York City provided additional details regarding the degree to which African Americans and Latinos disproportionately bear the brunt of pot-law enforcement. Their study found that African Americans accounted for more than half of all marijuana arrests in New York City for the years 1997 to 2007, though they represented only 26 percent of the city's population over that time span. Hispanics accounted for 31 percent of those arrested on pot charges, though they represented only 27 percent of the population. By contrast, whites accounted for only 15 percent of those arrested, despite being 35 percent of the city's population.[17]

Equally troubling is the disproportionate enforcement of marijuana laws upon young people. According to NORML's 2005 report, 74 percent of all Americans busted for pot are under age thirty, and one out of four are age eighteen or younger.[18] That's nearly a quarter of a million teenagers arrested for marijuana violations each year.

Looking beyond these startling statistics, it is apparent that the disproportionate enforcement of America's marijuana laws has psychological implications as well. The imposition of pot prohibition alienates millions of otherwise law-abiding citizens to believe that the police and civic leaders are instruments of their oppression rather than their protection. This policy, at best, creates widespread disrespect for the rule of law and, at worst, threatens the long-term stability of society.

5. Drug dealers don't card—the criminal enforcement of marijuana prohibition has inadvertently made it easier for kids to buy pot.

Ask any advocate of marijuana prohibition why they oppose legalization and you will almost always receive the same response: Keeping pot illegal keeps it out of the hands of children. In fact, according to the White House Office of National Drug Control Policy, the primary reason pot is outlawed today is to prevent young people from trying it. Unfortunately, America's cannabis policies do not achieve this goal.

According to the University of Michigan at Ann Arbor, which has tracked data on teen pot use since the mid-1970s, more than 85 percent of teenagers say that marijuana is "fairly easy" or "very easy to get." Shockingly, this percentage has not significantly changed in over thirty years, despite the government's increased emphasis on marijuana-law enforcement, arrests, and interdiction efforts over the past two decades. What has changed? Government surveys indicate that teens are now trying cannabis at younger and younger ages.[19] Something else has changed over the past three decades, too. Tellingly, more teenagers now claim it is easier for them to purchase weed than beer or cigarettes.[20] There is one primary reason for this trend: Drug dealers, since they are not acting legally as part of a regulated market, do not ask for IDs when they make sales to young people.

Naturally, proponents of prohibition counter that the number of teens smoking pot would inevitably be even higher if marijuana were regulated like alcohol. Perhaps, but not necessarily. After all, lifetime use of cannabis by Dutch citizens aged twelve and older is less than half of what it is in America—despite that country's far more liberal marijuana policies.[21] Moreover, even in America most young people who refrain from cannabis don't do so out of fear of the law or an inability to score. Rather, they choose not to use pot simply because they don't like feeling high.[22] In other words, marijuana prohibition, or the lack thereof, plays little to no role in their decision.

6. **Regulating marijuana would make the drug safer because consumers would be aware of the product's quality, purity, and potency.**

As we've articulated previously, cannabis—by virtually any measurable standard—is a relatively safe drug, especially when compared to the health risks associated with other intoxicants or prescription medications. That said, marijuana is not without some physical and psychological risks. Chief among these are tachycardia (a rapid increase in heart beat) and paranoia. In almost all cases, these adverse reactions occur when the user unknowingly consumes marijuana of an unusually strong potency. Were cannabis to be legally regulated like alcohol—whereby pot producers and distributors would be mandated to clearly specify the drug's potency on the product's packaging—the likelihood of consumers experiencing such inadvertent "bad" reactions would no doubt fall considerably.

Regulating the production and sale of cannabis would also cut down, if not altogether eliminate, instances of so-called contaminated pot. Though rare, we are aware of occasional instances of unscrupulous drug dealers "padding" their marijuana with glass shavings and other potentially dangerous particles in order to weigh down individual bags of cannabis. (Pot is generally sold by weight in one-eighth, one-quarter, one-half, or one-ounce quantities.) Rarer still are instances where pot sellers will lace their wares with other psychoactive chemicals such as PCP or formaldehyde. These unethical actions on the part of unregulated drug sellers pose significant health risks to consumers, who have no way of knowing whether the quality of the product they are purchasing has been compromised. These practices would all but disappear if marijuana were legally produced and sold like alcohol—with government-regulated controls guiding every step of the drug's production, packaging, and sale.

7. **Marijuana prohibition, not the use of marijuana itself, creates the so-called gateway to other illegal drugs—and it also produces a dangerous criminal market.**

As we noted in chapter 5, few cannabis consumers ever go on to use other illicit substances. In many respects, this result is surprising. After all, the criminal prohibition of pot limits the selling of the drug exclusively to entrepreneurs who are willing to break the law. Naturally, many of these dealers also sell other, more dangerous products like cocaine and heroin. The more one visits such dealers and is exposed to these other products, the greater the likelihood that one will be tempted to try them.

Separating marijuana from the illicit drug market and regulating its sale in state-licensed stores, as society does with alcohol, would significantly reduce consumers' exposure to harder drugs and their temptation to experiment with them.

For those who defend marijuana prohibition as a means of "protecting kids," we ask that they consider this: By keeping cannabis illegal, our laws are steering young people into an underground market where they will be exposed to more harmful substances. It need not be this way. For example, in the Netherlands where the sale of cannabis is relegated to state-licensed coffee shops (which, by law, may not sell other, so-called hard drugs) rather than dimly lit street corners, less than 2 percent of the adult population has ever used cocaine.[23] By contrast, more than 16 percent of Americans have tried the drug.[24]

Finally, it should be noted, if not emphasized, that the criminal prohibition of cannabis also exposes consumers to more harmful people—as the drug's production and sale is primarily relegated to criminal enterprises and, increasingly, drug gangs. For example, as this book goes to print, violence is escalating on the Mexican border. Much of this violence, if we are to believe U.S. law enforcement officials, revolves around the actions of Mexican drug cartels. According to the Associated Press, marijuana is the "biggest source of income" for these ruthless drug gangs.[25] Legalizing and regulating cannabis like alcohol would eliminate this primary income source for these cartels and, in turn, eliminate much of the growing violence and turf battles that currently surround the drug's illegal importation from Mexico. Whether one consumes marijuana or not, this is a result we believe that all Americans would welcome.

———

As we stated in the beginning of this chapter, the promotion of these arguments by advocacy organizations has built a strong base of support for marijuana-law reform in this country. This, obviously, is a positive development. Yet, neither separately nor as a whole have these arguments ever convinced a solid majority of the American public to support the seemingly obvious conclusion that cannabis should be legalized, taxed, and regulated. Why is this the case? Our hypothesis is in the next chapter.

chapter nine

Not Adding a Vice but Providing an Alternative

After reading chapter 8, you are probably wondering how the government manages to justify keeping marijuana illegal. It is a good question. Clearly, the case for maintaining our current system of pot prohibition is specious at best. In fact, the evidence demonstrates that criminalizing cannabis produces far greater harm to society than the responsible use of marijuana itself. You would think then that a majority of the public, when presented with this evidence, would demand replacing cannabis prohibition with a system of taxation and regulation. Well, that is what one major marijuana-policy-reform organization thought, too.

In 2002, and again in 2006, the Marijuana Policy Project set out to prove that the arguments we presented in chapter 8 could convince an electorate to support regulating cannabis in a manner similar to alcohol. They launched their campaign in Nevada, home of legal gambling and legal prostitution. To twist the famous phrase about New York City, MPP apparently assumed "If you can't make marijuana legal here, you probably can't make it legal anywhere." But the organization was under no illusions. It knew that Americans' bias against marijuana was strong and that overcoming it would be no easy task—even in a libertarian-leaning state like Nevada.

In order to fully appreciate the Marijuana Policy Project's campaigns in Nevada, you need to know a bit about MPP. Put aside any preconceived notions you might have about longhaired hippies marching in the streets. The Marijuana Policy Project fits no such stereotype. Located on Capitol Hill in the heart of Washington, D.C., MPP employs more than thirty staffers—most of whom would be more likely to fit in at a K Street cocktail party than a pot rally—and possesses an annual operating budget of approximately $5 million. It has spearheaded successful statewide lobbying and initiative campaigns in numerous states—including Hawaii, Vermont, Maryland, Montana, Massachusetts, and Michigan—to enact significant changes in cannabis policy. In short, the MPP team works long hours, strives for perfection, and plays to win.

We share these insights about the Marijuana Policy Project to illustrate that the Nevada campaigns provided a legitimate test of the effectiveness of the traditional arguments in favor of repealing cannabis prohibition. MPP did not simply place these initiatives on the ballot and then hope for a positive outcome. Quite the contrary, they conducted an elaborately orchestrated and well-financed campaign to convince a majority of the public that we should treat pot like alcohol. According to the media and campaign-finance reports filed with the state, MPP spent approximately $1,800,000 in 2002[1] and about $2,800,000 in 2006.[2] Much of this money was used to purchase airtime so that voters would be exposed to MPP's best and most persuasive legalization arguments.

Many of these arguments were the same ones we summarized in the previous chapter. For example, one MPP ad asked voters whether the state should continue to "waste police resources enforcing marijuana laws that don't work or use them to go after those who would really hurt us," such as violent predators, murderers, and rapists. Another ad, featuring black-and-white, surveillance-style, nighttime footage of a man dealing marijuana on the street, argued that taxing and regulating pot would take it out of the hands of drug dealers, while simultaneously providing money to the state for education, roads, and other priorities. For good measure, MPP even ran an ad touting that their proposal would *increase* the penalties for certain drug-related crimes, such as driving under the influence of marijuana.

MPP also emphasized that Nevada voters had previously legalized the medical use of cannabis. One campaign ad depicted a medical marijuana patient lamenting that high school students could purchase pot relatively easily while state-authorized patients must struggle to find it. The spokeswoman in the ad argued that a regulated system of cannabis legalization would provide patients with safe and reliable access to their medicine. The tagline at the end of yet another commercial succinctly summarized the overall theme of MPP's advertising campaign: "Vote Yes on Question 7—a sensible alternative to our failed marijuana laws."

Despite MPP's powerful and pervasive messaging, a strong majority of Nevada residents voted, twice, to maintain the existing system of criminal prohibition. In 2002, the initiative garnered just 39 percent of the vote. Four years later, MPP's 2006 initiative was supported by 44 percent of the electorate. This was a significant improvement, but still well short of the majority needed for passage.

So if the residents of Nevada heard all of the standard arguments in favor of taxing and regulating marijuana like alcohol, what prevented them from embracing MPP's proposals? Our supposition is this: MPP's campaign rhetoric—and, more specifically, its ads—while logical and rational, were not designed to directly address the one core question that festers in the minds of many voters: "Why should we add another vice?"

You see, given the thesis of this book, the irony is that one of the primary reasons why citizens are denied the legal use of marijuana is because of alcohol—or, more specifically, because of the negative attributes associated with the abuse of alcohol. The American people are all too familiar with the range of alcohol-related problems described in chapter 7, from health care expenditures to lost productivity to reckless and violent behavior. While they are not clamoring for a return to alcohol prohibition and for the most part consider alcohol a fun recreational substance when used in moderation, they recognize that alcohol use does not come without significant costs. So logically—or at least it appears logical on the surface—people ask, "If alcohol causes so much damage to society, why should we encourage the use of another intoxicating substance?"

It is our contention that this single concern often outweighs all of the sound and rational arguments presented in chapter 8. Simply put, many Americans are afraid of the idea of adding the *perceived* dangers associated with marijuana to a society that is already reeling from the *known* harms associated with alcohol. Further, according to national and state survey data, approximately one-fifth to one-third of Americans consider pot to be *more harmful* than booze. Another one-third of the population believes that marijuana is at least as dangerous as alcohol. Stop to consider that for a moment. Given all that we know about the dangers of alcohol—many of which we've described in detail—there are still many, if not a majority, of Americans who mistakenly believe that weed is as bad as or even *worse* than booze. So is it really surprising that the public's support for marijuana legalization remains mired below 50 percent nationally?

Faced with this current reality, marijuana legalization advocates have two options. The first option is to demonstrate—in a far more powerful and convincing manner than they have so far—that the harms associated with the criminal prohibition of marijuana far outweigh the harms of marijuana itself. The second option, which we describe in the following pages, is to persuade the American people that the use of cannabis is not only *less* harmful than they currently believe, but that making it available to adults could actually *reduce* the use of a more harmful substance. To accomplish either one of these goals, but especially the latter, it is necessary to juxtapose the harms of marijuana against the harms of alcohol.

Marijuana Jujitsu: Using the Adverse Effects
of Alcohol to Our Advantage

One would think that marijuana legalization advocates would enthusiastically embrace the pot-versus-alcohol comparison. After all, when one steps back and objectively evaluates the potential risks of pot and booze, marijuana's side effects are relatively insignificant. Nevertheless, some advocates have been hesitant to make direct comparisons between the two substances, fearing that discussions about the harms of alcohol will only serve to remind the public that marijuana might pose similar detrimental effects. Others have been reluctant to position cannabis as a less harmful alternative to alcohol, assuming that making such a comparison might appear as if they are promoting marijuana use.

Interestingly, the same advocates who shy away from comparing the effects of pot to the effects of alcohol typically do not hesitate to compare marijuana prohibition to alcohol prohibition. Listen to almost any speech by a prominent drug-policy reformer and you are likely to hear a reference to the failure of America's so-called Noble Experiment. The purpose is to remind the audience that the federal prohibition of alcohol did not stamp out alcohol use; rather, it significantly increased the crime associated with alcohol and drove its use underground where the lack of regulations made its consumption more dangerous. Yet when reformers make this comparison, they downplay that the use of alcohol increased once Prohibition ended. Their goal is simply to convince the audience that prohibition is counterproductive, and since it was deemed a failure for alcohol, it should also be deemed a failure for marijuana.

Of course, whether it is emphasized or not, most everyone in the audience will assume that ending marijuana prohibition would increase the availability and use of cannabis, perhaps significantly. If this audience is made up of individuals already familiar with the relative harms of marijuana and alcohol, then the likely prospect of an increase in the public's use of pot will not necessarily be much of a concern to them. But if those listening believe that cannabis is potentially as harmful as alcohol—which is what most swing voters who will ultimately decide whether marijuana should be legal in the future are likely to believe—they will not be thrilled by the prospect of marijuana storefronts opening up in their neighborhoods. When you consider this fact, it becomes almost shocking that any advocate would *intentionally* avoid educating the public that marijuana has been proven to be less harmful than alcohol.

Instead of avoiding comparisons between pot and booze, we propose that proponents of marijuana legalization engage in some verbal jujitsu. Jujitsu is a fighting technique involving the use of balance and leverage to turn your opponent's strength and momentum to your own advantage. As things stand today, Americans' concern over the ill effects of alcohol—as exhibited by the question, "Why add another vice?"—is a force *against* marijuana-policy reform. Advocates for cannabis regulation want the public to accept legalization *despite* the fact that a substantial portion of the public considers marijuana to be at least as dangerous as alcohol. In short, reformers are calling for a society where adults will have legal access to alcohol *and* marijuana at a time when the public is becoming increasingly aware of the health and societal problems associated with booze. This is an uphill task to say the least.

Sure, it may be possible to legalize marijuana despite this sentiment, but it will not be easy. In order to turn the tide after more than seventy years of marijuana propaganda and prohibition, the American people must be *inspired* to change the status quo. But if they believe—or are allowed to continue to believe—that the legal access to cannabis for adults will only compound many of the alcohol-fueled problems our society already faces, they will support keeping the system the way it is. This is where we need to apply our jujitsu. We will take our opponents' strongest argument—that alcohol is associated with a wide variety of social ills—and twist it to our advantage. How will we do this? By responding to our critics, over and over again, that we are not seeking to add a vice. Instead we are providing adults with a safer and less harmful recreational alternative to alcohol.

In sum, the fact that alcohol causes so many problems in our society is not a reason to keep pot illegal; rather, it is *the* reason we must make it legal. Unless our opponents are going to argue for a return to alcohol prohibition, they will be forced to explain why they wish to compel adults to use the more harmful recreational intoxicant.

So Can You Put This in an Equation?

We are glad you asked. In order to better convey the rhetorical and strategic advantage of using the "marijuana is safer than alcohol" message, we have created what we believe to be the first-ever equation to predict whether an individual will be willing to support the establishment of a legally regulated marijuana market. In our "mind of the marijuana user" equation an individual will support marijuana legalization if:

$$(\text{Desire to use} - \text{current ability to use}) + \text{desire to avoid negative consequences of marijuana prohibition} + \text{perceived benefits of reform} > \text{Perceived benefits of marijuana prohibition} + \text{desire to avoid negative consequences of reform}$$

To summarize: We believe there are factors that steer people toward supporting marijuana legalization and other factors that drive them to oppose it. Weighing in on the pro-legalization side are individuals' desire to use cannabis without the fear of punishment, their perception of the benefits that would stem from marijuana-law reform, and their desire to avoid the negative consequences of pot prohibition. Working against the cause of legalization are individuals' perceptions regarding the benefits of the current policy and their expectations of the potential negative consequences of regulation.

Up to now, the intellectual debate over whether to legalize cannabis has dwelled almost entirely upon the *negative aspects* of this equation. The government emphasizes the potential negative consequences of reforming the status quo, and advocates of more liberal marijuana laws stress the negative consequences of the current policy. Unfortunately, as we describe below, this is a dynamic that chiefly benefits opponents of pot-law reform. But if we break down this equation, you can see how comparing the relative harms of alcohol and marijuana can transform the marijuana legalization debate in a way that greatly enhances the cause of reform.

Factors That Strengthen One's Support of Marijuana Legalization

The desire to use – current ability to use

The first part of the equation is a tabulation of the public's self-interest. Simply put, how strongly does an individual want to use marijuana legally? For many Americans, regardless of whether they have used pot previously or not, this desire may not exist at all. For others—current users especially—the desire to use marijuana may be quite strong. But this does not necessarily mean that this latter group will be ardent advocates for legalization. This is because they may already be able to access and use marijuana as much as they wish without any serious threat of punishment. If their current ability to use cannabis is roughly equal to their desire to use it then their score on this part of the equation will be close to zero and their passion for reform—despite the very real enjoyment they derive from marijuana—may end up being quite low.

On the other hand, while the purpose of this book is not to promote or encourage the use of cannabis, there is no denying that the federal government's antipot propaganda has steered many Americans away from it. As a result of this demonization campaign, millions of Americans have never stopped to consider whether they might be better off from a health perspective if they used marijuana instead of alcohol. A public education campaign about the relative harms and benefits of the two substances, such as we are advocating, could conceivably have the net effect of raising "desire to use" scores. This is true both for individuals who have used marijuana in the past and for those who have never tried it. By contrast, campaigns based on the more traditional arguments for reform do not drive up "desire to use" scores.

The desire to avoid negative consequences of prohibition

If individuals are going to support marijuana law reform, they must believe that there are negative consequences associated with the status quo. Traditional reform advocates have generally focused all of their attention on this part of the equation in their attempts to build majority support for legalization. They frame the issue by appealing to one's sense of justice ("Patients who need marijuana shouldn't have to find their medicine on the streets") or by articulating the current law's impact on society as a whole ("Prohibition has created a dangerous criminal market," or "We are wasting law enforcement resources arresting marijuana users"). This is the strategy MPP employed in Nevada in 2002 and 2006.

While these arguments are effective in the sense that they can marginally drive up an individual's score on the pro-reform side of the equation, the reality is that this rhetoric may not be particularly persuasive for many Americans. For example, some Americans may believe, in theory, that it is a waste of law enforcement resources to go after individuals for possessing small amounts of pot. However, they may be dubious that these efforts legitimately prevent police from combating more serious crimes. Likewise, many Americans may believe that our society would benefit from the revenues derived from the sale of marijuana. That said, their support for legalization may still be offset by their concerns about the perceived negative consequence of more widespread marijuana use.

In order to dramatically increase the public's scores on the pro-reform side of the equation, proponents of marijuana regulation must make a much stronger case that marijuana prohibition is producing definite negative outcomes. We can do this by explaining how the prohibition of marijuana, a recreational alternative that is less harmful than alcohol, is literally driving Americans to drink. In turn, the widespread—and encouraged—use of alcohol increases the likelihood of domestic abuse, sexual assault, and other forms of violence and is producing serious negative health outcomes, including overdose deaths. In other words, our current laws are perpetuating a society that is demonstrably less safe for our sons and our daughters. This personalizes the debate. The question is no longer whether voters can live with the negative consequence of misplaced law enforcement priorities, for example; it is a question of whether they want their children living in a world where acts of violence are more likely. We believe that this message can ultimately help tip the scales in favor of legalization.

The perceived benefits of reform
Not surprisingly, individuals will be more likely to support marijuana legalization if they believe specific benefits will occur as a result. The benefits we refer to here are societal benefits, as opposed to the personal benefits we previously quantified in the "desire to use" factor of the equation. In a societal sense, the perceived benefits of reform are in many ways the flip side of the negative consequences of the current policy. For example, it would be a benefit to society as a whole if criminal justice resources were directed away from marijuana law enforcement and toward investigating more serious crimes. Similarly, it would be a major societal benefit if we were to diminish the strength and reach of drug cartels and gangs by eliminating a major source of their revenue. But legalization would do far more than simply bring an end to the undesirable consequences of prohibition. It would also produce one major benefit: a taxed and regulated marijuana market would likely generate billions of dollars that could be used for programs like education or drug and alcohol treatment. With respect to this benefit, we must note, there is not a tremendous advantage for the "marijuana is safer" message compared to the traditional arguments—as either strategy can allude to the allure of a tax-revenue windfall.

There is one other notable potential benefit of reform—related to the theme of this book—but it is far more subjective and not quite ready for prime time, so to speak. This is the notion that an increase in marijuana use will actually have a positive impact on our society. While we support the "marijuana is safer than alcohol" mantra and argue that there is little reason to fear responsible adults using marijuana, we think that it would be a stretch to say that most swing voters will initially view the prospect of more citizens using cannabis instead of alcohol as a positive benefit—even if it they understand that pot is a safer alternative. In the long run, however, once marijuana use is more open and accepted in our society, we believe many citizens will come to appreciate that cannabis tends to foster a more peaceful and enjoyable environment than does alcohol. But this epiphany is likely a ways down the road. For now, the strength of our message is not that it necessarily encourages voters to celebrate pot's positives aspects, but rather, as we discuss below, that it undermines our opponents' arguments as they attempt to exaggerate the negative consequences of legalization.

Factors That Weaken One's Support of Marijuana Legalization

The perceived benefits of prohibition
Shifting to the other side of the equation, the first factor we must consider is the perceived benefits associated with prohibition. Obviously, if support for the status quo is strong, one is unlikely to endorse changing it. In general, those who support marijuana prohibition perceive two primary benefits. First, many Americans believe the current system dissuades kids and adults from using marijuana by limiting their access to it. Second, and far less charitably, some Americans believe that consuming cannabis is amoral behavior and, therefore, those who use the drug deserve to be punished—or at least sent to treatment so they can be "cured of their addiction."

There is no question that this is the most difficult part of the equation to affect. This is true with respect to both traditional arguments for cannabis-law reform as well as arguments based on a "marijuana is safer than alcohol" message. If a person is antimarijuana to his or her core and believes the most important goal of any public policy is to prevent people from using cannabis at all costs, then trying to persuade this person to support a legal, regulated system will be a tough sell. That said, the appreciation that cannabis is less harmful than alcohol could potentially soften the person's visceral opposition to the plant, and possibly diminish his or her enthusiasm for punishing marijuana users.

The desire to avoid negative consequences of reform
The final factor in our equation is typically our opponents' ace in the hole. When it comes to influencing this part of the mental equation, marijuana prohibitionists believe that anything goes. They understand that many Americans fear any change to the status quo and use this fact to their advantage by alleging that taxing and regulating pot will lead to innumerable adverse consequences—many of which we outlined (and rebutted) in chapter 5. All of these allegations serve to trigger and deepen the underlying concern that legalizing marijuana would be "adding another vice" to our society, and promote the belief that cannabis is an especially dangerous vice.

To make matters worse, legalization advocates have essentially allowed their opponents to set the terms of the marijuana policy debate. Prohibitionists claim "marijuana is evil"; legalization advocates say it isn't. Prohibitionists claim "marijuana is a gateway drug"; legalization advocates say it isn't. Prohibitionists claim the use of marijuana use will lead to the downfall of society; legalization advocates say it won't. And on and on it goes. Sure, these myths can be refuted—reformers rebut these and similar allegations day in and day out—but the government will always have a much bigger megaphone.

To summarize this entire back-and-forth, we have a situation in which prohibitionists have asserted that marijuana is a dangerous vice and legalization advocates have, at best, spent years trying to prove that it is not as bad a vice as they claim. Yet advocates' rebuttals to these accusations do little to soothe the minds of voters who still consider marijuana a harmful drug and believe more people will use it if it becomes legal. Reformers simply hope that the public's objections to prohibition will outweigh these fears. But by approaching the subject this way, advocates are making their task needlessly more difficult than it could be.

Injecting the subject of alcohol into the marijuana legalization debate provides two significant benefits, each of which serve to reduce the public's concerns about the potential negative consequences of reform. First, framing the perceived harms of marijuana relative to the known dangers of alcohol demystifies the plant by providing voters with a familiar point of comparison. Absent this point of reference, people unfamiliar with pot have no way of knowing whether to believe the government, which implies that cannabis is extremely harmful, or drug-law reformers, who suggest that it is less so. This is the environment in which the marijuana debate has taken place in the past and, as a result, reformers have engaged in fruitless and endless debates about how dangerous marijuana may or may not be. For example, many reform advocates would consider it a "victory" to finally, after more than twenty years, convince a majority of Americans that marijuana is not a "gateway drug." And what would be the advocates' reward for this "victory"? They could spend the next decade rebutting the allegation that more teenagers are in treatment for cannabis than any other drug. In short, no matter how logical or how persuasive reformers' rebuttals are, antimarijuana zealots will always have new talking points ready and waiting.

Using alcohol as a point of reference immediately blows this game apart. The harms of marijuana are no longer left to the public's imagination, with the government encouraging nightmarish visions. Instead, members of the public are now able to fix a point along the continuum of harms—the point where each individual person places alcohol—and advocates of marijuana-law reform are able to argue that pot's potential dangers fall far below it. Once this shift occurs, almost all of the government's claims about the alleged dangers of marijuana seem utterly ridiculous. The possibility that the use of marijuana might very slightly increase the risk of mental illness does not seem so scary when compared to the fact that 35,000 Americans die each year from alcohol consumption. Similarly, framing the legalization debate in this manner makes it far more difficult for elected officials to defend their desire to punish marijuana users. Unless they are equally willing to demand the arrest and imprisonment of adults who use a more harmful substance that is far more likely to contribute to sexual assault, domestic abuse, and other acts of violence, their bias becomes embarrassingly obvious.

Beyond demystifying the plant, infusing talking points about the relative dangers of alcohol into the marijuana legalization debate will also enable reformers to respond more effectively to opponents' claims that the public's overall use of pot may nominally increase under a system of taxation and regulation. As we noted earlier, this is a subject reformers generally try to avoid discussing out of the fear that acknowledging the possibility of any increase in marijuana use would be perceived to be a negative consequence. By reframing the debate and demonstrating to the American people that legalizing marijuana would not be "adding a vice," but instead would be providing adults with a less harmful recreational alternative, advocates can discuss these potential trends without being defensive. Thus, the potential for increased marijuana use by adults would not be measured against current levels of cannabis use; rather, it would be measured against current alcohol use. Instead of pushing for a system that encourages what is currently considered a "negative consequence of reform" (increased marijuana use), reformers would be increasing awareness about and fighting to reverse a "negative consequence of current policy" (widespread alcohol use). It is this rhetorical and substantive difference that we believe will ultimately tip the debate over marijuana legalization in favor of reform.

chapter ten

From Theory to Practice: "Safer" to SAFER

Well, it all sounds rather simple, doesn't it? Convince the public that marijuana is less harmful than alcohol and the battle to legalize cannabis will be over. A marvelous plan in theory, but how does one implement this strategy in practice? Unless you are the drug czar's office, you can't promote your message via a national advertising campaign. In fact, with a novel idea like this, it is often difficult to raise the money necessary to even fund a *local* advertising campaign. Donors tend to limit their giving to established organizations and programs with demonstrated success.

No, for this public education effort to be successful, it will require the help of hundreds of thousands or, more likely, millions of Americans. By "help," we don't mean full-time or even part-time employment or volunteer work. Nor do we mean providing financial assistance to our respective marijuana-policy reform organizations (although such assistance would be more than welcome). Rather, we expect that the advocacy efforts of those inspired by this book will be limited to spreading the gospel through personal interactions with friends and family.

But we know that some of you may still be skeptical of the persuasiveness of this message, and desire hard evidence showing that it is actually effective in practice. It is for this reason that we have included this chapter. In the pages that follow, we will describe how a campaign based on the "marijuana is safer than alcohol" argument redefined the entire cannabis debate in a state of nearly five million people. Ridicule turned to seriousness, dismissiveness evolved into acceptance, and opponents were silenced or, in some cases, even turned into supporters.

In a sense, this campaign demonstrates on a grand scale what any individual can accomplish among family members, friends, or classmates. For those of you who are inspired to speak out after reading about these efforts, we provide suggestions in chapter 11, as well as in a special appendix at the conclusion of this book, explaining how to advance the campaign message in ways both large and small.

In the summer of 2004, Steve Fox (one of this book's coauthors) was the federal lobbyist for the Marijuana Policy Project. He had been working for the organization since 2002, with the primary responsibility of convincing members of Congress that they should prohibit the U.S. Drug Enforcement Administration from circumventing state medical marijuana laws. While he fought that battle vigorously, his passion rested in the bigger picture. He aspired to see the day when it was legal for *all* adults to use marijuana without the threat of criminal punishment or arrest. Driven by this interest, he became an avid reader of survey data collected by MPP in advance of its state-based reform efforts. His goal was to understand exactly which factors, arguments, and beliefs prevented a majority of the American people from supporting the legalization of marijuana.

Studying the cross-tabs in these surveys, he noticed an interesting trend. When participants were asked whether marijuana was more harmful, less harmful, or as harmful as alcohol, responses tended to be divided equally among the three choices. About a third of those polled believed cannabis was safer than alcohol, while a third believed pot to be more dangerous than alcohol. The remaining third of respondents reported that they believed the two drugs were equally dangerous. Comparing these responses to the participants' support of regulating, taxing, and selling marijuana like alcohol, he found that support for legalization became more widespread as the harmful effects that respondents' perceived in the use of cannabis decreased. In fact, among the one-third of respondents who considered marijuana to be less harmful than alcohol, support for legalizing marijuana tended to be around 75 percent.

Fox believed that these opinion polls held significant implications for marijuana-law reform. First, they demonstrated that those who understand—perhaps through their own personal use—that marijuana is a relatively benign substance, especially as compared to alcohol, are naturally more inclined to support making it legal. Second, they indicated that much of the public remains unaware of the objective fact that pot is far less harmful than alcohol. With these thoughts in mind, Fox believed that support for marijuana-policy reform would increase significantly if the truth about the relative harms of pot and alcohol could be more effectively conveyed to the public.

To test this hypothesis, he proposed that the Marijuana Policy Project provide grant funding for a campus-based effort to advance the "marijuana is safer than alcohol" message. Launching this campaign on college campuses seemed to be the best strategic choice given the widespread popularity of both substances among students. Students are also quite familiar with the problems associated with alcohol use—from fights to vandalism to sexual assaults. As originally envisioned, the project was going to be dubbed the "High and Dry" campaign, a reference to what would be promoted as a healthier way to party.

MPP agreed to fund the project and recruited Mason Tvert (another coauthor of this book) to head the campaign. As his first move, Tvert proposed a new name for the campaign—Safer Alternative for Enjoyable Recreation, or "SAFER." It proved to be a perfect name with which to convey the campaign's message.

In January 2005, the SAFER campaign was officially launched on the campuses of Colorado State University (CSU) and the University of Colorado at Boulder (CU). These universities were not randomly selected. Just a few months earlier, each campus had experienced a tragic alcohol-overdose death of a young student. This virtually guaranteed that the campaign's message would resonate with the public and would spark an important debate. With luck, the leaders of the campaign hoped, it would even generate some media coverage in the local papers. Not in their wildest dreams did they anticipate the reaction they received.

SAFER decided that the most effective way to spark attention would be to coordinate student ballot initiatives on both campuses, enabling students to weigh in on the following question: "Given the fact that marijuana is objectively less harmful than alcohol, should the penalties on campus for the use or possession of marijuana be no greater than the penalties for the use or possession of alcohol?" While these referenda were not binding, the assumption was that they would, if adopted, manifest the support of the student body and send a strong message to the broader community. Almost from their inception, the initiative campaigns generated a stream of publicity. And it was not just the campus newspapers covering the story. At one point, when student leaders at CU threatened to kick SAFER's question off the ballot, local television network affiliates covered the action. Most importantly, the vast majority of news stories contained, in some fashion or another, the message, "marijuana is less harmful than alcohol." In the end, majorities of students on both campuses voted in favor of the initiatives.

Having achieved success on college campuses, SAFER decided to take its campaign to the next level by running a citywide initiative in Denver. The initiative proposed eliminating all penalties for the adult possession of up to one ounce of marijuana. The organization collected the 5,000 signatures needed to qualify for the ballot and launched a campaign based on the theme, "Make Denver SAFER." In every single public pronouncement, SAFER stuck religiously to its basic message. Tvert, who was the public face of the campaign, rarely uttered a sentence without the words "marijuana" and "alcohol" included. In order to provoke controversy and generate additional media coverage, SAFER encouraged an allied organization to erect a billboard featuring the face of a battered woman and the message: "Reduce domestic and community violence. Vote YES on I-100." This action spurred a two-week-long debate in the media about alcohol's role in encouraging violent behavior and whether the legalization of cannabis would reduce incidences of domestic abuse.

SAFER also generated headlines with a campaign targeting Denver Mayor John Hickenlooper, who opposed the initiative. Because the mayor had made his personal fortune as a beer brewer and brew-pub owner, SAFER displayed a large banner outside his office posing the question: "What is the difference between the mayor and a marijuana dealer?" The answer, as it appeared on the banner: "Mayor Hickenlooper deals a more dangerous drug." The YouTube clip of Tvert calling the mayor a "drug dealer" for the first time during a live interview on the Fox affiliate—causing the anchor to do a cartoonlike double-take stutter—remains a SAFER favorite to this day.[1]

Opponents of the Denver initiative were clearly thrown off-stride by SAFER's unconventional strategy. No longer did their efforts to demonize marijuana resonate as powerfully as they once did in the minds of the public. When responding to critics, Tvert readily acknowledged that marijuana was assuredly not harmless, but argued that it was certainly less likely than alcohol to lead to domestic abuse, sexual assault, and other acts of violence. He challenged his opponents to explain the logic behind prohibiting adults from using a substance objectively less likely to be detrimental to the public's health and safety. One city councilman who opposed SAFER's efforts became so frustrated with the campaign he resorted to ripping "Make Denver SAFER" signs out of the ground and throwing them away—an act of vandalism that he later admitted to on television.

On November 1, 2005, the SAFER team, content that it had succeeded in its mission of stimulating a citywide debate about marijuana on its terms, gathered at a local bar (irony noted) to watch the returns come in. Expecting about 40 percent of the vote, the first shock came when the absentee ballots—which typically represent older, more conservative voters—came in well above that figure. As the Election Day results trickled in, the percentage in favor of the initiative continued to rise. By the time all of the votes had been counted, the initiative had garnered almost 54 percent of the vote. Denver had become the first city in the United States to eliminate *all* penalties for the adult possession of marijuana! The victory produced some incredible icing on the public-education cake, as Tvert was able to take the SAFER message national, with appearances on numerous national news outlets, including Fox News and MSNBC.

In the weeks that followed the Denver victory, the hands of fate steered SAFER toward its next endeavor. Law enforcement authorities in Denver, with the apparent backing of the alcohol-dealing Mayor Hickenlooper, announced they would continue to cite marijuana offenders *under state law*. They were not required to do so, but made a calculated decision to ignore the will of the public. Faced with this intransigence, SAFER announced in December 2005 that it was launching a statewide initiative campaign in Colorado to change the state's marijuana-possession law. The next morning, a front-page banner headline in the *Rocky Mountain News* screamed, "State Pot Law Push." In the article, Colorado attorney general John Suthers said he looked forward to a "head-on, outright debate about legalization."[2] This was music to SAFER's ears.

After collecting more than 130,000 raw signatures, SAFER was ready to roll out its campaign in support of "The Alcohol-Marijuana Equalization Initiative," also known as Question 44. The language of the initiative, similar to the Denver initiative, sought to make the possession of up to one ounce of marijuana legal for individuals twenty-one years of age and older. Again, it is important to note that SAFER had no illusions about winning this campaign. Sure, the

Denver campaign surprisingly ended up in SAFER's favor, but there seemed to be little chance the more conservative parts of the state would provide the margin needed to produce a statewide majority. Accepting defeat as a likely outcome, SAFER's goal was to use the campaign to generate, on a very limited budget, widespread earned media coverage containing the "marijuana is safer than alcohol" message. In essence, the statewide campaign would serve as a public-education vehicle designed to make the Colorado more fertile ground for future statewide initiatives or legislation.

During the Question 44 campaign, SAFER promoted its message to every part of the state. The organization erected billboards and held events in Boulder, Fort Collins, Grand Junction, Colorado Springs, and elsewhere. One SAFER billboard, featuring a bikini-clad model lying under the words, "Marijuana: No Hangovers. No Violence. No Carbs!" was the talk of Denver. As campaign spokesperson, Tvert was able to pen op-eds for the *Denver Post* and the *Rocky Mountain News*, exposing tens of thousands of readers to the "marijuana is safer than alcohol" message. And he participated in a televised one-on-one debate against the state attorney general (who got the statewide debate he wanted). In the final week of the campaign, SAFER and NORML organized a mass protest outside of an anti-44 event sponsored by the governor and law enforcement. Speakers at the event were drowned out by more than one hundred of marijuana-law reform advocates chanting, "Hey, hey. Ho, ho. You say drink. We say no!"

The statewide campaign also provided SAFER the opportunity to take on the federal government. SAFER mocked a White House antidrug ad that claimed that "nothing" happens when one smoked marijuana[3] by erecting a billboard claiming that even the drug czar's office concedes that cannabis is the "safest thing in the world." As luck would have it, then–drug czar John Walters arrived in Denver to speak out against the Colorado ballot initiative the same day that SAFER unveiled its new billboard. This serendipitous occurrence not only ensured widespread coverage of the billboard, but also forced the drug czar to spend the day talking about whether marijuana was really the safest drug on Earth.

During the final week of the Question 44 campaign, SAFER learned that both President George Bush and Vice President Dick Cheney would be visiting Colorado. The SAFER team immediately designed and placed newspaper ads humorously pointing out the negative role alcohol had played in Bush and Cheney's lives and suggested that this was "one more reason" to vote yes on 44. SAFER's ad featuring a photo of Cheney alongside the text "Shot his friend in the face after drinking" became the most e-mailed photo on Yahoo! News for more than forty-eight hours. The impact of the ads extended all the way to Air Force One, where a White House spokesman, the late Tony Snow, dismissed them as "kind of snarky and juvenile."[4] Perhaps. But there is no question that the SAFER message had penetrated to the highest echelons of our government.

As expected, Election Day 2006 passed without the victory SAFER had enjoyed in Denver. That said, the SAFER team was far from disappointed. A Mason/Dixon survey taken just one month earlier had found only 34 percent of respondents in favor of the initiative. Yet when all the votes were counted, the initiative ended up with a very respectable 41 percent of the vote. And within the city limits of Denver, support for marijuana legalization, as measured by election results, increased from 53.5 percent in 2005 to 54.5 percent in 2006.

Following the statewide loss, SAFER conducted the third and final act in its Denver-oriented electoral trilogy. In 2007, the organization placed an initiative on the Denver ballot to make the enforcement of marijuana-possession laws the city's "lowest law enforcement priority." Such LLEP initiatives had succeeded in a number of other cities in the United States, most notably Seattle, where arrests for pot possession had fallen dramatically following enactment of the law. In theory, passage in Denver would increase pressure on local police to stop focusing their time and resources targeting adult cannabis consumers. The initiative also sought to establish a "Marijuana

Policy Review Panel" to study marijuana- and alcohol-related incidents in the city to determine the impact of each on the community.

In the end, the LLEP initiative attracted a healthy 57 percent of the vote in November 2007. Following its passage, the review panel, which included representatives from the Denver police, the city council, and the district attorney's office, along with proponents of the initiative, public defenders, and other interested individuals, initiated regular meetings. At one of the panel's first meetings, members adopted a recommendation calling on the city to stop citing adults for marijuana possession in compliance with the voters' wishes. Given the make-up of the panel, this recommendation was not unexpected. The surprise, however, came days later, when the *Rocky Mountain News*, which had opposed every SAFER effort up to that time, echoed the panel's call in an editorial. Here is their own explanation of how the SAFER-influenced public opinion affected their own position: "We opposed both measures. After the first one passed we even said it would be wrong for police to stop enforcing the state law against marijuana possession. But given the unambiguous sentiment in Denver to end these prosecutions, we've since concluded that the city should back off on this matter."[5]

This was not the first time a SAFER-led effort had produced a shift in tone in the major media. Following the initial 2005 ballot victory, the *Denver Post* published a lengthy article about mothers who use marijuana. It appeared on the front of the paper's "Scene" section accompanied by a large color photo of a woman in the shadows of her garage smoking marijuana from a pipe.[6] A number of quotes in the article directly echoed the SAFER message. One woman offered: "[Marijuana] is fun. It's a way to connect. It's like having a beer with someone. It's less harmful than alcohol, it's not fattening, it's ultimately cheaper. Alcohol is so bad for your body." Another mother said of her daughter, "I'd much rather have her smoke pot than drink because she'll be much less likely to get into bad situations." It is quite likely statements like this had never appeared in a major U.S. newspaper before.

In 2009, the Denver city attorney's office announced that marijuana prosecution fell over 20 percent from 2007 to 2008. In both a symbolic sense and a literal sense, the "marijuana is safer than alcohol" message had proven effective. In short, a powerful, persuasive, logical, and effective message, backed by a small staff and limited resources, had persuaded the media, the public, and even members of law enforcement and government to consider a new reality. The world has not changed yet, but the walls—in Denver especially—have certainly started to crumble. In the next chapter, we will describe the steps you can take to knock down some bricks in your own community.

chapter eleven

Toward a Tipping Point: Creating a Buzz—and Sparking Change

We know the battle ahead will be long, but always remember that
no matter what obstacles stand in our way, nothing can withstand
the power of millions of voices calling for change.
—BARACK OBAMA, JANUARY 8, 2008

Are you with us?

As we stated in the opening of this book, we assume—in fact, we hope—that not all of you reading this are necessarily strong supporters of establishing a legal and regulated marijuana market. Many of you no doubt are, but we recognize that some of you may be reading this book more out of curiosity than anything else. Or perhaps someone encouraged you to read it and you are merely humoring him or her. If that is the case, then it is likely that after a lifetime of half- or whole-hearted opposition to marijuana use, you picked up this book with a great deal of skepticism. At this point, however, we hope that you are thinking about cannabis a bit differently than you did before. Perhaps you are beginning to appreciate why some adults would want to consume marijuana recreationally. More significantly, perhaps you are even beginning to believe that they *should* be allowed to do so legally. Of course, this does not necessarily mean that you are ready to publicly share your evolving beliefs with the members of your book club or your weekend softball team. In fact, you may assume, at least initially, that your newfound pot perspective is going to be your "dirty little secret." If that is the case, you may have little use for this chapter.

For everyone else, we have provided this chapter to arm you with the words and phrases you will need to advance the "marijuana is safer than alcohol" message in your community. SAFER's campaigns in Denver and on college campuses nationwide have demonstrated that this message resonates with the mainstream media and at the ballot box. We've initiated the conversation. Now it is up to you to continue the dialogue with your friends and family.

Collectively, every conversation and action you engage in that conveys the "marijuana is safer than alcohol" message brings us closer to a "tipping point"—a point in time signifying when an idea becomes conventional wisdom. Sociologist Malcolm Gladwell describes a tipping point as "the moment of critical mass, the threshold, the boiling point" at which an idea, trend, or behavior takes off, goes viral, and becomes a social epidemic.[1]

In our case, it is critical that those who already understand the relative harms of pot and booze begin spreading the "marijuana is safer than alcohol" message to others. By doing so we will eventually reach our own tipping point—a time when the question of whether marijuana or alcohol is the more harmful substance is no longer debatable in conventional society. Marijuana will simply be viewed, as it should be, as less harmful than alcohol. At that point, changes in our nation's irrational marijuana laws and policies will be inevitable.

Starting Small—Engaging in Conversations with Your Friends and Family

Assuming you are now ready to wake your colleagues out of their "alcohol is acceptable; marijuana is not" stupor, how should you go about it? One option, of course, is to buy them copies of this book. Yes, we know this advice sounds like we are just trying to boost our sales, but can you blame us for trying?

Kidding aside, we expect that most of you will be less direct—and a little more frugal—in your outreach and educational endeavors. Instead of dropping this book in your friends' laps, you will more than likely begin by dropping verbal hints, subtle references, and some relevant facts about the relative dangers of marijuana and alcohol when the opportunities arise. We recognize, however, that even these small exchanges can feel intimidating when one is dealing with a taboo subject like pot. While it may not be as difficult as telling your parents that you just flunked out of school or confessing to your significant other that you were unfaithful, we can see why you may still be hesitant. So we would like to offer you a few words of encouragement.

The first thing to keep in mind is that you are essentially just sharing facts. While these facts ultimately serve to enhance a specific position—that the use of marijuana should be legal for adults—you can decide for yourself how far you want to go in terms of engaging in that policy debate. In most cases, you need not engage in that debate at all. For example, if you happen to find yourself in a conversation about the rising number of sexual assaults on college campuses, you could mention that university presidents have acknowledged that most of these incidents are alcohol related and very few, if any, are caused by marijuana. If the person responds by saying something like, "Well, that's probably because those friggin' stoners are too lazy to do anything," you can just shrug off the ignorant comment and change the subject. All that really matters at this point in the game is that the person with whom you were speaking was exposed to evidence reinforcing the message that marijuana is less harmful than alcohol. At some later time, once people like this have heard the same message repeated from a variety of sources, they will have to look inward and reconcile why they continue to support laws that steer adults toward a substance that is far more dangerous than cannabis.

Of course, not everyone will respond in such a hostile manner. Many people, including those who disagree with you, will want to continue the conversation. Fortunately, unlike many other debates you will engage in during your lifetime, this is a situation where the facts are almost entirely on your side. Sure, your opponents may have some valid concerns regarding if and how marijuana should be sold in a regulated market—we address these concerns in detail in the following chapter—but there is really no way they can defend the position that marijuana is objectively more harmful than alcohol. Once one contrasts the two drugs' impact on mortality (35,000 annual deaths in the United States from alcohol consumption; zero from marijuana), emphasizes alcohol's far greater association with sexual assault and domestic abuse, and adds for good measure that alcohol is about twice as addictive as pot, well, there is not much left for someone on the pro-booze side to say. (And if somebody brings up a common myth about pot, you will know how to respond to that, too, since you have read chapter 5.)

As an added boost to your confidence, let us share a little secret with you. When you finally overcome your reluctance to discuss this controversial subject openly, you are likely going to discover something surprising: More people agree with you than you previously assumed. Of course, having been conditioned by society to oppose and ridicule any discussion regarding marijuana or marijuana policy, most of them will not be overly enthusiastic in their support. But you can expect to hear a fair number of people saying, "Yeah, you're probably right." Some folks may even share their own observations about the social ills associated with alcohol versus the relative peacefulness associated with marijuana.

One final caveat: Be aware that even those people who acknowledge that marijuana is less dangerous than booze may be reluctant or unwilling to concede that pot should be legal. After more than seven decades of marijuana prohibition, it is hard for many people to envision anything else—at least at first. If this is the case, don't worry. For now your mission is simply to engage in a discussion about the relative harms of the two substances—and on that point, your position is unassailable.

Arm Yourself with Simple Responses to Common Antimarijuana Assertions

As any good Boy Scout knows, it is always best to be prepared. Fortunately, we are in a position to aid your preparations. Collectively we have, without exaggeration, engaged in *thousands* of conversations about marijuana—its uses, its effects, and why we need to reform the laws that criminally prohibit its use by adults. Based on our experience, we can fairly accurately anticipate how others will respond when you raise the subject. So here are some recommended ways to incorporate the "marijuana is safer than alcohol" message into your conversations. We have even highlighted a few "money quotes" that will help you win any debate decisively.

When someone says: "Alcohol is bad enough. Why should we add another vice?"
You reply: "We would not be adding a vice; we would be allowing adults the option to choose a less harmful alternative for relaxation and recreation. Currently, laws intentionally steer Americans toward the use of alcohol when many of these citizens would prefer to use a far less dangerous substance, marijuana.

When someone says: "So you want more people using marijuana?"
You reply: "Not necessarily, but I do believe that adults should have the legal *choice* to use whichever substance they prefer. It simply doesn't make sense to punish adults who make the rational choice to consume the less harmful of the two substances.

When someone says: "I just don't like the idea of more people using marijuana."
You reply: "What bothers you so much about the notion of an

adult using marijuana responsibly in the privacy of his or her own home? Are you equally bothered by the idea of an adult using alcohol under these same circumstances? If not, why not? Why would you rather have adults solely consuming alcohol?"

When someone says: "Well, I don't agree that people should use either substance."
You reply: "We are not going back to alcohol prohibition. Alcohol, just like marijuana, is here to stay. The only question to debate is whether our society should keep steering people toward booze or whether we ought to allow adults legal access to a less harmful alternative that is far less likely to lead to violent and destructive behavior."

When someone says: "Okay, so maybe pot is less dangerous than booze. But smoking marijuana is still illegal."
You reply: "Well, maybe it shouldn't be. Tens of millions of Americans use marijuana. Do you really think it makes sense to put these people in jail or to waste law enforcement resources and court time issuing and processing citations? Why should our laws *punish* adults who choose to use the less harmful substance?"

When someone says: "But won't legalizing marijuana make it more available to children?"
You reply: "How much more available could marijuana be? Marijuana prohibition has created a situation in which more than 85 percent of high school seniors say it is 'very easy' or 'fairly easy' to obtain, and nearly one out of two high school seniors has tried it. It is hard to imagine a system, including one of legalization, that would create an environment where our children have even greater access to marijuana than they already do."

When someone asks: "But aren't you concerned that you're sending the wrong message to kids?"

You reply: "Lying about the relative dangers of pot and alcohol, as our social and criminal policies do now, is sending the wrong message to our children. We are misinforming our kids that alcohol is safer than marijuana. That message has literally killed thousands of teenagers and will continue to cause countless more deaths. We recognize that kids are exposed to both substances, and the truth is that we don't want adolescents using either one. But we don't do them any favors by creating the false impression that alcohol is safer to consume than marijuana. Even putting aside the multitude of societal problems associated with alcohol use—like violence and sexual assault—the truth is that teenagers can die from an alcohol overdose. That is simply not possible with marijuana. Yet some surveys show that teens falsely believe that it is safer to binge drink than to use cannabis. We must be honest with kids about the relative harms of the two substances, while discouraging the use of either one."

When someone says: "Yeah, but if we make marijuana legal, we are going to have more lazy stoners sitting around doing nothing."
You reply: "That is just a stereotype. Millions of Americans enjoy marijuana occasionally at dinner parties or other gatherings with friends. Their behavior is no different than the way many adults consume alcohol. To say that every marijuana user is a lazy stoner is the same as saying that every person who drinks is overly aggressive and is likely to cause harm to himself or others."

When someone says: "I basically agree with you, but I don't want more 'stoners' out on the streets."
You reply: "What is it about an adult using marijuana responsibly that makes you so uncomfortable? If you were walking down the street at night with a friend, would you prefer to encounter a group of men who had been drinking or a group of guys who had been smoking marijuana?"

Money Quotes

- We would not be adding a vice; we would be giving adults the option to choose a less harmful alternative for relaxation and recreation. Currently laws intentionally steer citizens toward the use of alcohol, when many of them would prefer to use a far less harmful substance, marijuana.
- I believe that adults should have the legal choice to use whichever substance they prefer. It simply doesn't make any sense at all to punish adults who make the rational decision to consume the less harmful of the two substances.
- What bothers you so much about the notion of an adult using marijuana responsibly in the privacy of his or her own home? Would you be equally bothered over the idea of an adult using alcohol in this same situation? If not, why not?
- Why would you rather have adults consume alcohol?

Raising the Subject

Now that your confidence is brimming and you are armed with the rhetoric you need to effectively rebut almost any counterargument, you may wish to proactively engage others in conversations about the relative harms of marijuana and alcohol. You may even want to raise the question of why our laws more severely punish those who engage in the use of the less harmful of these two substances. At the same time, you may be hesitant to raise the subject at the Thanksgiving table right after someone has asked you to pass the mashed potatoes. We don't blame you. That's why we encourage you to wade into the subject more slowly, bringing it up after others have initiated a marijuana-related conversation. Fortunately, you will likely find that the subject of pot comes up more often than you previously noticed. Here are some common examples:

Developments in the political and legislative arenas. With incidents of drug-related violence on the U.S.-Mexico border becoming more frequent and more frightening, mainstream political commentators are starting to raise the issue of legalizing marijuana as a means of shutting off a source of drug-cartel funding. The possibility of legalizing marijuana to increase U.S. tax revenues is also popping up in the news more and more often. Medical marijuana is another subject frequently in the news, as many states work on implementing their existing medicinal cannabis legalization systems, while other state legislatures consider adopting laws of their own.

Suspensions of athletes for possessing or using marijuana. Just during the writing of this book, there were a spate of pot-related punishments in the National Football League, the National Basketball Association, and, of course, the world of Olympic sports, a few of which we detailed in chapter 6. Some of these players had no prior disciplinary actions in their career, yet they were harshly punished nonetheless. Of course, had any of these players been out drinking at a club instead there likely would have been no disciplinary action taken at all.

Busts of celebrities for marijuana possession. Unlike pro athletes, celebrities aren't likely to be suspended from the Screen Actors Guild if they're busted for weed. That said, you can be certain that the mainstream media will publish embarrassing headlines—and perhaps even a police booking photo—when a well-known individual is unfortunate enough to get caught with a little marijuana. This was the case in 2004, when Art Garfunkel of the famous singing duo Simon and Garfunkel was found with marijuana in his jacket when his driver was pulled over for speeding. Garfunkel is hardly alone. Other celebrities busted for pot include Oliver Stone, John Lennon, Paul McCartney, Dennis Hopper, Mick

Jagger, Neil Diamond, Dionne Warwick, Carlos Santana, Joe Cocker, David Lee Roth, Bob Denver and Dawn Wells (Gilligan and Mary Ann from *Gilligan's Island*), and the late Tupac Shakur (while he was in jail, no less!).

Politicians' children running afoul of marijuana laws. If a young person is cited for marijuana possession—and hundreds of thousands of young people are each year—it is not mainstream news. If that young person happens to be the son or daughter of an elected official, that is news. Al Gore III, the son of the former vice president, learned this lesson the hard way in 2003 when he was pulled over for driving without his headlights on and police officers discovered a baggie of marijuana. [Elected officials take note: We know that the younger Gore is hardly the only child of a prominent politician to smoke an occasional joint, so you may want to support legalizing the safer choice before you are publicly ridiculed as a hypocrite.]

Marijuana-related incidents in your community or on your campus. There have been more than twenty million marijuana-related arrests in the United States since 1965. Therefore, it is likely that someone you or your family knows will have a marijuana-related run-in with the law at some point in his or her life. It's equally likely that someone you know at your university will get in trouble for marijuana possession. Either situation provides you with an opportunity to publicly defend someone in your community who has been inappropriately punished for making the rational choice to use a less harmful substance.

Alcohol-related incidents in your community or on your campus. If you truly wish to take advantage of the unique nature of the marijuana-versus-alcohol subject, begin to inject the topic into conversations about alcohol-related incidents. Not surprisingly, you will find these opportunities occur frequently. Bar fights, celebratory riots after professional or college sports championships, disruptive and drunken behavior at sporting events, out-of-control fraternity or off-campus parties, and news about professional athletes getting arrested for violent behavior after a night of drinking (which is an all-too-common occurrence) are all incidents that can serve as a starting point to initiate a conversation about the folly of steering Americans toward alcohol use and prohibiting them from using cannabis instead.

Going Public

Like Barack Obama said during his campaign for the presidency, there is no denying "the power of millions of voices calling for change." But he also demonstrated during that twenty-two-month journey that those voices need a leader, or leaders, to inspire, unify, and mobilize them, and turn their collective passion into political power. It is our hope that many of you reading this book will want to lead a similar call for change on your campuses and in your communities. If you are one of these budding leaders—or if you are already a prominent figure in your community and wish to begin driving home the "marijuana is safer than alcohol" message—please be sure to check out the appendix, which provides a detailed list of suggestions about how you can help build this movement.

chapter twelve

Our Vision of the Future

Imagine driving home one Friday evening. The weekend is here; it's time to put the daily grind of the 9-to-5 workweek behind you. You grab a DVD at the local movie rental store and, before heading home, you decide to purchase some items to enhance your viewing experience. After running into the corner convenience store for a bag of chips and some soda, you make one final stop—the marijuana shop, so that you can pick up a couple of grams of locally grown cannabis.

Behind the store counter are several varieties of marijuana. Each bears a readily identifiable name and possesses its own unique flavor and potencies. You are well aware of each strain's strength and effects, as well as whether it was grown with or without the use of pesticides, because all of this information is clearly displayed on the packaging label. Once you make your selection, the cashier asks for your identification. Upon showing him or her your driver's license or some other form of state-issued ID, the clerk verifies your age and rings up your purchase. You drive the rest of the way home knowing that tonight is going to be a "highly" enjoyable and relaxing evening—and confident that you won't be waking up Saturday with a hangover.

Does this situation sound far-fetched? It shouldn't. In many ways—and in many places—this scenario is closer to reality than you might think.

Defining What We Mean When We Say "Legalization"

Before we can articulate to you what our vision of a legally regulated system for the sale and use of cannabis would look like, we must first define what we mean when we use the term "legal market." After all, without proper context, this phrase can mean entirely different things to different people. Oranges are legal. So are alcohol and tobacco. Aspirin is legal, as are thousands of prescription medications—including highly dangerous drugs like oxycodone. Yet while all of these products are "legal"—in the sense that they may be lawfully produced and purchased by certain consumers—their distribution and possession are governed by vastly different regulatory controls.

Oranges, for instance, are widely available to *all* consumers, regardless of age. People can even grow their own, if they so desire. Aspirin is also readily available to the general public as an over-the-counter medication, whereas prescription drugs may only be purchased at a state-governed pharmacy by those who possess written authorization from a licensed physician. Federal and state regulators closely monitor the sale and use of prescription substances, and impose strict criminal sanctions upon both doctors and pharmacists who dispense them inappropriately.

The sale of alcohol and tobacco are also legal, yet both substances are heavily taxed and tightly controlled. State-imposed age restrictions place limits on who can legally purchase and use both products, and federal laws also specify how and where these products may be advertised. (Tobacco companies cannot market their products on television or display outdoor billboards in close proximity to schools, for example.) Federal, state, and county laws also impose strict controls regarding where these products can be legally purchased. For instance, some states do not allow alcohol to be sold in gas stations, convenience stores, pharmacies, or supermarkets. Other states allow for the sale of some types of alcohol (such as beer) in certain locations (such as supermarkets), but restrict the sale of other types of alcoholic beverages (such as gin or rum) to specially licensed liquor-only stores.

Adults may legally produce certain types of alcohol, like beer and wine, privately in their home—if their production is intended for their own personal consumption and not for sale to the public. By contrast, federal and state laws tightly regulate the commercial production of any type of alcohol.

Every state imposes restrictions regarding which days, or which times of day, consumers may purchase alcohol—in Connecticut, an adult can't buy booze after 8 p.m. or on Sundays or federal holidays, for example—and some states, like Pennsylvania, even impose limits on the quantity of alcohol a person may legally purchase at one time (state-licensed distributors must sell beer by the case). State and local laws also restrict where the consumer may legally use alcohol. For instance, most states prohibit any use of alcohol inside a vehicle or in a public setting such as a state park or beach. Further, even venues that legally permit alcohol consumption on their premises, like bars and restaurants, can refuse to serve patrons who they believe are sufficiently intoxicated or pose a danger to themselves or others. Finally, some parts of the United States (so-called dry counties) have chosen to outlaw the sale of booze altogether.

As evident above, rules regulating the sale and use of many legal products, and alcohol in particular, are complex and vary greatly according to state and local laws. Nowhere in the United States is booze legal in the same manner that oranges and chewing gum are legal. In virtually all cases, the laws regulating the drug's possession, sale, and use are designed to reflect cultural mores, maximize public safety, and discourage abuse—particularly among young people. We propose that similar standards should govern the regulated sale and use of cannabis.

So What Would a Legal, Regulated
Marijuana Market Look Like?

In some respects, we already have a fairly good idea. State-licensed coffee shops in the Netherlands have legally sold small amounts of cannabis to patrons eighteen years of age or older for more than two decades. While Dutch lawmakers have made minor adjustments to the law over time—for instance, limiting the quantity of cannabis that consumers may purchase to no more than five grams, and imposing restrictions on the number of licensed coffee houses that may operate in communities that reside near the country's borders—few have ever suggested repealing the government's long-standing legalization model.

How does the Dutch system work? It's fairly simple, actually. Consumers of proper age who possess a valid ID may legally enter a coffee shop, which typically resembles a conventional bar or café. Once inside, patrons may elect to either sit at a table or at the counter, where they may order any number of cannabis-based goods (most coffee shops dispense pot in both herbal or edible preparations) from a bartender or waiter. Customers select the item or items they desire from a menu (the menu provides information on the types of marijuana available—including its potency and intoxicating effects—as well as its price) in a manner that is little different from how most of us would order a beer or a sandwich at a popular restaurant. ("What's the specialty of the house?" one might ask; or "What do you recommend?") After placing their order, the waitstaff brings the desired items to the patrons, who may elect to consume their marijuana on the premises—like most traditional bars or cafes, most coffee shops offer a variety of foods, beverages, and live entertainment—or take it home with them for later use.

While many Americans are somewhat familiar with the Dutch system described above, far fewer realize that there are other examples of legal cannabis regulation available closer to home. Notably, in California hundreds of storefront businesses dispense cannabis openly to authorized consumers (those who possess a physician's written recommendation) in accordance with state and local laws. (Similar operations also exist—though on a far more limited basis—in Canada, where the medicinal use of marijuana is legal under federal law, as well as in Oregon and Colorado, where medical cannabis use is also permitted under state law.) Like most other commercial enterprises, California's medical marijuana facilities (more commonly referred to as "dispensaries" or "cooperatives") must be locally licensed, pay state and municipal sales tax, and abide by community zoning regulations. For example, in most cities, cooperatives are not allowed within close proximity to schools or churches, and their frontage must refrain from displaying any overt references to the cannabis plant. Entry to these facilities is limited only to those who possess proper authorization, and a patron's identification is typically verified at the door. Would-be customers who fail to show a valid doctor's note or a state-issued medical-marijuana identification card to the dispensary's door manager are not allowed inside the premises.

The floor plan of an American cannabis dispensary varies from business to business. Some establishments are designed to closely resemble the look and feel of a traditional medical pharmacy, while others are designed like a café or coffee house—replete with couches, chairs, and tables so that patients may congregate and socialize. In most California dispensaries, cannabis-based products are inconspicuously located in a separate room away from the store's main lobby area. (Other facilities provide patrons with an illustrated menu and do not display their products out in the open at all.) At least one or two staff members, commonly known as "budtenders," are available to answer patrons' questions regarding the numerous types of marijuana-based products offered for sale and their effects. Like in the Netherlands, California dispensaries typically sell marijuana in a variety of preparations, including herbal cannabis, edibles, and tinctures. However, unlike in the Netherlands, most dispensaries do not allow patrons to utilize cannabis on the premises.

Many of the rules and standards governing the sale of marijuana in California have developed over time. Prior to the passage of statewide medical marijuana legalization in 1996, a handful of communities—such as San Francisco, Oakland, and Los Angeles—acted on their own to implement local ordinances legalizing the establishment of cannabis cooperatives. Following the passage of the California Compassionate Use Act of 1996, additional dispensaries began operating all throughout the state—though these facilities were not technically legal under state law until some years later. California's legislature eventually codified the sale and distribution of cannabis by licensed businesses in 2004. By 2008, even California's attorney general had issued formal guidelines articulating legal business practices for the distribution of cannabis by dispensaries. These guidelines were incorporated after legislators engaged in extensive meetings with representatives from the patient community and dispensary owners. A handbook outlining "best business practices" for the community-based distribution of cannabis is also available on the Internet.[1]

Moving Beyond the Dutch and California Models

In the paragraphs above we have described two models of de facto legal cannabis distribution. (We use the term "de facto" because even in the Netherlands the commercial production of cannabis—even cannabis that is grown for sale in licensed coffee shops—is technically illegal, though seldom prosecuted. In the United States, federal laws still prohibit large-scale cultivation in California and other states.) In both cases, these models operate with solid political and public support. Equally important, in both the Netherlands and in California, neither regulatory model has been associated with dramatic increases in cannabis consumption by unauthorized users or by young people. Lifetime cannabis use among Dutch adolescents, though it has risen slightly over the years, remains significantly lower than among U.S. teens, and in California marijuana use among young people *declined* sharply following changes in state law.[2] In short, these regulatory schemes are functioning primarily as legislators and the public intended, and abuses of the system have been kept to a minimum. Even in California, where some critics have called for stricter regulations for cannabis providers, police report that the state-sanctioned distribution of marijuana has "not greatly affected their law enforcement activities" nor has it led to "routine" misuse by the public.[3]

As you can see, many of the guidelines outlined in the previous section are remarkably similar to those that already govern the distribution and consumption of alcohol. There is one core difference, however. The commercial production of alcohol is licensed, taxed, and regulated, whereas the commercial cultivation of cannabis—even in California and the Netherlands—is unregulated and still remains, at least technically, illegal.

It doesn't have to be this way, of course. Many countries already license private manufacturers to legally cultivate marijuana for public and commercial purposes. For instance, most European nations, as well as China, Australia, and Canada, have enacted regulations allowing for licensed farmers to grow industrial varieties of marijuana (hemp) as an agricultural product. Commercial farmers in these countries obtain a government permit to plant, grow, and harvest cannabis, which they then sell at a profit to private manufacturers.

Some nations even license private businesses to produce psychoactive strains of cannabis. For instance, GW Pharmaceuticals—a biotechnology firm based in the United Kingdom—is permitted by the British Parliament to cultivate tens of thousands of marijuana plants. (Cannabinoids from the plants are eventually extracted and used in marijuana-based medicines, which are then sold by the company on the worldwide market.) Additionally, both the governments of Canada and the Netherlands license private firms to supply high-quality cannabis for those nations' medical-marijuana programs.

(Under Canadian and Dutch law, authorized patients may obtain medical marijuana for a fee from the federal government.)

Of course, no nation has yet to license commercial businesses to manufacture and distribute marijuana in a manner similar to the production and sale of drugs like alcohol or tobacco, but that's not to say that the government couldn't do so. During World War II, the U.S. government licensed farmers to grow marijuana commercially for industrial purposes. Certainly federal officials could license commercial producers to cultivate cannabis for recreational purposes as well. Or, if the feds aren't comfortable getting into the pot production business they could simply choose to do nothing at all and let the individual state governments decide how best to implement local laws and procedures overseeing the legal production of cannabis. In many ways, this is what is happening today with state-sanctioned medical-marijuana programs, most notably in California.

Pot Sales: Who, Where, and When?

As with the sale of alcohol or tobacco, commercial sales of cannabis should be limited to designated venues. Like liquor stores, such venues would be subject to community zoning laws, and their access would be restricted only to those of legal age.* Businesses authorized to sell cannabis that failed to abide by these standards would face strict sanctions, such as fines, loss of their business license, as well as possible criminal penalties. Cannabis-based

---

*While we recognize that all U.S. states currently restrict the sale and use of alcohol, aside from the use of wine during religious services, to those age twenty-one and over, we are not convinced that the imposition of this somewhat arbitrary age limit has been particularly productive at limiting the drug's access or safeguarding public health. As a result, we would prefer to see age restrictions on the sale and use of marijuana to be based on community standards. Were a specific age requirement to be imposed, we would favor limiting the purchase of cannabis to those who are at least eighteen years of age. We believe that this age requirement, while also in some ways arbitrary, is more consistent with current attitudes and societal standards—as persons eighteen years old may already legally enter binding contracts, marry, vote, serve in the military, and purchase tobacco.

products sold to the public would be mandated to carry visible warning labels highlighting the product's intoxicating effects (e.g., "An adult should not operate a motor vehicle or heavy machinery after consuming marijuana") and potential risks to health (e.g., "Women who are pregnant or nursing should not consume marijuana"), as well as information about the product's THC content and potency. These labels should also indicate to the consumer whether the cannabis being sold was grown organically or with the use of pesticides. Finally, venues that sell cannabis should also be legally authorized to market marijuana paraphernalia, such as grinders, pipes, vaporizers, or other related products pertaining to the adult use of cannabis.

Any commercial marketing of cannabis via public advertising campaigns would arguably be subject to federal, state, or local restrictions, just as marketing of tobacco and some alcohol products is limited to forums that have limited exposure to young people. For instance, advertising the sale of a commercial brand of cannabis on television or radio before 11 p.m., or in the pages of certain types of magazines or newspapers, could be prohibited. Cannabis sales to consumers could also be restricted to certain days or hours of the day, as is already the case with alcohol. Communities would also be free to place limits on the number of venues licensed to sell cannabis, or to prohibit the establishment of such venues entirely.

As with alcohol, the public consumption of cannabis in any location aside from private residences and designated venues—such as adults-only marijuana smoking facilities (if such facilities were permitted under local law)—would most likely be discouraged. Those who violate public no-smoking laws would face sanctions ranging from civil fines (for consumption in a public park or on a street corner) to more severe penalties (for public use in a vehicle or on school property), including potential criminal charges. In short, laws allowing for the legal use of cannabis, like booze, should not permit its use whenever and wherever one chooses.

Under the system we are proposing, private employers would

still have the discretion to prohibit their employees' marijuana use on company time, and to sanction (or fire) employees who arrive to work under the influence of cannabis—just as they currently do for alcohol. If an employee is suspected of being impaired by marijuana while on the job, an employer would maintain the ability to drug-test him or her "for cause." Presently, many businesses already engage in such testing. For example, many construction companies will insist that employees undergo post-accident blood testing, which—unlike urinalysis—can better determine whether someone has consumed marijuana (or other drugs) in the previous few hours (as opposed to the previous few days). Employers can also utilize impairment testing, which measures one's ability to perform certain physical or simulated tasks, to identify whether an employee has recently consumed cannabis, and take appropriate action if it is determined that he or she has.

Finally, the manufacturing and sale of cannabis by licensed companies should be subject to taxation. State and local taxes would apply to cannabis sold at state-licensed retail outlets, just as these same taxes apply to the sale of alcohol, tobacco, and gasoline now. Licensed manufacturers and retailers of cannabis would also be subject to state and local sales tax on their profits, like all other commercial businesses. How much revenue could such a system produce? As we noted in chapter 8, by some estimates the federal legalization of pot could reap over $30 billion annually. Ideally, portions of this newfound revenue could be redirected to federal and state public health programs to pay for drug treatment and education efforts, much like how "sin" taxes imposed on tobacco products are currently used to pay for antitobacco advertising.

Of course, imposing regulatory and licensing requirements on the commercial production and sale of cannabis would not necessarily restrict the activities of the small-time "home grower." Just as America's alcohol regulations allow for the unlicensed, private production of home brew by adults, we believe that individuals should also be able to legally engage in the noncommercial production of cannabis without having to obtain a government license or pay a state or federal surcharge. That said, it is likely—even under a system of cannabis regulation—that many consumers will *not* decide to consistently grow their own herb, just as most Americans choose not to consistently grow their own vegetables or brew their own beer. Rather, we believe that most marijuana consumers, like most adults who drink alcohol, will elect to purchase cannabis products produced by a licensed, regulated manufacturer and sold at a state-sanctioned store.

Discouraging Marijuana Use and Driving

As we discussed in chapter 5, marijuana's adverse impact on psychomotor skills is less severe than that of alcohol. Nevertheless, driving under the influence of cannabis still poses an elevated risk of accident. As adults begin to have greater access to marijuana in a legal, regulated setting, we must ensure that the public is also exposed to a consistent message discouraging the use of pot prior to driving.

Just as public education campaigns targeting the use of alcohol have significantly reduced incidences of drunk driving by the general public, we believe that a similar high-profile effort should also be directed toward discouraging the use of cannabis and driving. Public service campaigns targeting drugged-driving behavior should be aimed particularly toward those aged eighteen to twenty-five—as this group is most likely to use cannabis, as well as to report having operated a motor vehicle shortly after consuming pot. In addition, this population has less driving experience, is generally more prone to engage in risk-taking behavior, and may be more naïve to pot's psychoactive effects than older, more experienced populations. Arguably, this campaign would enjoy enhanced credibility if coordinated by a private-public health association or traffic safety organization, such as the American Public Health Association or the AAA automobile club, as opposed to the drug czar's office—whose previous public service campaigns have demonstrated embarrassingly limited influence among younger audiences.[4]

Once the adult use of cannabis is legal, increased efforts should be made by law enforcement to train officers as drug-recognition experts so that they can better identify motorists who may be operating a vehicle while impaired by marijuana. The development of cannabis-sensitive technology to rapidly identify the presence of THC in drivers, such as a roadside saliva test, would also assist police in their efforts to better identify intoxicated drivers. It is our belief that the development of such technology, in addition to contributing to the public's safety, would also strengthen public acceptance for the taxation and regulation of cannabis by helping to assuage concerns that liberalizing marijuana policies would negatively affect traffic safety.

"But What about the Children?"

In the preceding sections we've tried to explain what a regulated system for the distribution, sale, and use of cannabis by adults would look like. Yet we know that some of you reading this book may remain concerned about the potential impact that such a system might have upon young people's attitudes toward marijuana. For instance, might teens perceive cannabis differently than they do now if its use and sale were legal for adults? And could such a taxed and regulated market, even with appropriate safeguards in place, inadvertently provide teens with greater access to marijuana than they have now? As two of the three authors of this book are parents, we understand these concerns and wish to address them.

As mentioned previously, implementing legal yet restricted access to cannabis is not necessarily associated with increased marijuana consumption among young people. (To repeat, marijuana use by young people *fell* in California following the enactment of laws allowing for the sale of cannabis to qualified adults.) Let us explain why we believe this is the case. One, even under our current system of criminal marijuana prohibition, almost 90 percent of teenagers report on government surveys that marijuana is easy to get. In fact, many high school surveys indicate that teens can more readily purchase illicit cannabis than buy alcohol or tobacco, both of which are legally available to adults but cannot be sold to children. One study by the National Center on Addiction and Substance Abuse (CASA) even reported that 23 percent of teens said that they could buy pot in an hour or less.[5] That means nearly a quarter of all teens can already get marijuana about as easily—and as quickly—as a Domino's pizza! In truth, no system we can think of could possibly provide our children with greater access to cannabis than the system we already have in place: prohibition.

That said, we are not going deny that some young people will still gain access to marijuana under a regulated system, just as some young people today have access to alcohol. Of course those who do will be obtaining a regulated product of known quality that is sold from a state-licensed retail outlet. This scenario, while hardly ideal, is still far better than the situation that exists today where millions of children are purchasing an unregulated product of unknown quality from millions of unlicensed sellers who have a financial incentive to encourage their customers to use other illegal substances like cocaine or methamphetamine. And don't forget, under our current system of prohibition teens don't even need to possess a fake ID to buy pot.

Truth be told, however, we do not assume that most teens, or even a strong majority of young people, will suddenly crave marijuana if it were legally available for adults. Virtually every teenager can already get his or her hands on cannabis now if he or she chooses. Yet it is apparent that most young people who quit using marijuana, or that never use it in the first place, abstain from it *despite* possessing the means to readily obtain it. For example, in 2008, investigators at the University of Michigan's Institute for Social Research reported, "The reason for not using or stopping marijuana use cited by the *fewest* [emphasis ours] seniors over the 29 years of data ... was availability (less than 10 percent of seniors)."[6] The authors further discovered that the artificially high price of cannabis on the black market, as well as young people's "concern about getting arrested," seldom influenced their choice whether or not to use marijuana.

By contrast, researchers reported that young people's "concern for psychological and physical damage, as well as not wanting to get high, were the most commonly cited reasons for quitting or abstaining from marijuana use." In other words, it's not the illegality of cannabis that dissuades teens from using it. Rather, it's adolescents' personal like or dislike for the intoxicating effects of cannabis, as well as their perceptions regarding its health effects, that ultimately shape their decision to smoke marijuana.

But isn't it possible that legalizing a substance that is currently prohibited might change the way some teenagers think about marijuana? Yes it's possible, but not likely. Tobacco is legal, even for some teenagers, yet cigarette use has fallen among young people to all-time lows because adolescents have become more and more aware of its health hazard.[7] Moreover, the *only* federal government study ever to evaluate the attitudes and use patterns of young people and marijuana in states that liberalized its possession determined, "Overall, the preponderance of the evidence which we have gathered and examined points to the conclusion that decriminalization has had virtually no effect either on the marijuana use or on related attitudes and beliefs about marijuana use among American young people."[8]

Talking to Your Children about Marijuana

In 2007, one of the authors of this book was asked to assist in updating a drug education curriculum known as *Safety First: A Reality Based Approach to Teens and Drugs.*[9] This curriculum is now taught in a handful of high schools and junior high schools in the United

States. Much of its focus is on how parents can talk openly and honestly to their children about marijuana, and by doing so, provide their teens with the skills and the confidence to make sound and safe decisions regarding the use of alcohol, pot, and other intoxicants.

The core tenets of *Safety First* are:

- provide honest, science-based information;
- encourage moderation if youthful experimentation persists;
- promote and understanding of the legal and social consequences of drug use; and
- prioritize safety through personal responsibility and knowledge.

As a society we incorporate these tried-and-true concepts when educating adolescents about the use and abuse of alcohol and tobacco. Unfortunately, adults too often fail to employ these same principles when it comes to marijuana.

Much of this neglect stems from marijuana's arbitrary illegal status. After all, the U.S. government, which sponsors much of the drug education that is taught in public schools, improperly maintains that *all* marijuana use is, in fact, abuse—even when it's consumed by adults in moderation in the privacy of their own homes. As a society, we do not typically discuss the use of alcohol in such an inflexible manner, nor should we. Rather, we explain that alcohol may be consumed responsibly, but only when used at the appropriate time, place, and in moderation.

Further, we make it clear that the use of alcohol, while acceptable for adults, is often inappropriate for young people, many of whom lack the maturity to responsibly engage in the use of a mind-altering substance. (Though when doing so, we acknowledge that many adults also lack the maturity to engage in a healthy relationship with booze.) And finally, we explain to young people that there are clear distinctions between alcohol *use* and alcohol *abuse*, and we provide teens with the skills to properly delineate the two behaviors. By doing so, we hope that our children will refrain from the use of alcohol—or at the very least, the irresponsible use of alcohol—and that they will seek help and assistance when they or someone they love is engaging in a dangerous, abusive relationship with the drug. We believe that these same principles should apply to the way parents discuss the subject of marijuana.

Fortunately, we believe that a regulated system of cannabis legalization will make it easier, not harder, for parents to rationally discuss this subject with their children. After all, many parents who may have tried pot during their youth (or who continue to use it occasionally) will no longer perceive societal pressures to lie to their children about their own personal habits. Rather, just as many parents today speak to their children openly about their use of alcohol, we believe that parents will finally be unburdened to talk objectively and rationally to their kids about pot. Perhaps some of them will even cite this book and its message in their discussions. After all, we wrote this book to evoke a public discussion, and we can't think of a more fitting and appropriate setting to begin this dialogue than at the dinner table.

Toward a Safer Future

Having spent the majority of this book encouraging you to think about marijuana as a safer alternative to alcohol, we would be remiss if we didn't conclude with a few thoughts about how the legalization and regulation of cannabis might change our alcohol-dominated culture. Here is the short answer: We don't know how it will change. As the legal use of marijuana has never been an option in modern America, it is difficult to predict how many people will choose to reduce their alcohol consumption in favor of pot once they are free to do so. Similarly, it is difficult to predict how many or how quickly doctors and other health professionals will feel comfortable encouraging or advising certain individuals under their care to substitute marijuana for alcohol. Will cities liberally grant zoning permits to establishments that want to serve marijuana (by vaporizer, most likely) as part of a dining, dancing, or movie-going experience—similar to the way establishments serve alcohol today—or will that develop very slowly? Will local law enforcement and university officials permit the use of marijuana during pregame tailgating so that celebrants have a nonalcoholic recreational alternative, or will such public use remain off-limits? With respect to these and many other similar questions, we simply do not know.

Here's what we do know. When marijuana is legal, an abusive husband or boyfriend somewhere in America will realize that he is better able to control his temper when he ingests pot instead of alcohol and will cut down on the Budweiser and switch to the kinder bud. Some college student we will never hear about will choose to use marijuana one night instead of joining his fraternity brothers in a drinking contest—thus avoiding a potentially tragic trip to the hospital that was otherwise fated to happen. When marijuana is legal, a man well on his way to chronic and eventually fatal liver disease will conclude that he wants to live a longer and healthier life and will voluntarily give up the booze in favor of pot. A young woman will decide to smoke cannabis and watch a movie one evening instead of going out drinking with her girlfriends, unknowingly missing a sexual assault that would have occurred after she had consumed one gin and tonic too many. By the very nature of introducing the less harmful recreational substance, marijuana, into the stream of commerce, probability dictates that these things will happen. Not just once, but hundreds and thousands of times. When marijuana is legal, we *will*, collectively, be safer.

Now go give this book to someone who needs it.

Spreading the "Marijuana Is Safer" Message

As we noted at the end of chapter 11, a movement cannot be successful without leaders to guide it. And we don't mean leaders on a national level; we mean hundreds or even thousands of activists at the grassroots level who are willing to engage with their friends and neighbors and organize activities. We are hoping that many people who read this book will be inspired to take on such a role and promote the "marijuana is safer than alcohol" message on their campuses or in their communities. We know from experience that it is not only fulfilling work, but it is also a great way to meet new people. If you are one of these budding leaders, here are some suggestions about ways to get active.

Getting Active on Your Campus

Colleges and university campuses provide an ideal environment for promoting the "marijuana is safer than alcohol" message. As we explained in previous chapters, many college campuses are all too familiar with the serious problems associated with alcohol use, and most students recognize that these same problems are not associated with marijuana use. Marijuana-policy reform also tends to be a uniquely popular issue among students (perhaps because so many students have firsthand experience with pot), and many have ample time and energy to invest in working toward it. Here are some pointers to help you capitalize on this fertile environment.

Start or Join a Student Organization

Although it is certainly possible to spread the "marijuana is safer than alcohol" gospel on your own, we strongly suggest that you consider joining or launching an official student organization. Such organizational status is often required to carry out certain activities on campus—such as hosting campus forums—and in some cases it comes with benefits such as free printing and copying, access to student activity funding, and campus office space.

You should begin this process by looking into whether there are any existing marijuana or drug-policy reform organizations already on campus—such as a chapter of the National Organization for the Reform of Marijuana Laws (NORML). If so, consider becoming involved with these groups and inquire whether they would be interested in launching a "marijuana is safer than alcohol" campaign. If there isn't already a likeminded organization on your campus—or if there is, but it's focused on other efforts—consider starting a new student organization. It's not as hard as it may seem, and there are numerous national organizations like SAFER and NORML that can help guide you in this process. (Contact information for these groups is included at the end of this appendix.)

Spreading the Message and Raising Funds

The easiest way to spread the "marijuana is safer than alcohol" message is to distribute flyers and other educational materials on and around your campus. You can simply download materials from the SAFER Campuses Web site (www.SAFERcampuses.org) or you could coordinate with SAFER to receive stickers and T-shirts, which you can use to raise funds to support your efforts. Find out whether your school has rules for distributing materials, and whether you are able to set up an information table in a high-traffic location on campus (typically inside or outside your student union). Whether you're tabling or just roaming campus handing out flyers, be sure to bring a clipboard so that you can collect the names and e-mail addresses of individuals who are interested in getting involved or learning more about your student organization.

Organize a Referendum

An extremely effective way of sparking a debate on campus over the relative harms of marijuana and alcohol is to place a referendum question on your school's student election ballot. Such a measure should express the sense of the student body that marijuana is less harmful than alcohol and, therefore, campus penalties for pot possession should be no greater than the penalties for illegal possession of booze. Although student organized campus referenda are typically nonbinding, they succeed in raising the profile of the issue and provide a specific goal around which you can organize. Referenda can usually be placed on the ballot either by petitioning the student body and collecting a minimum number of signatures, or by an action of your student government. Look to your student government office, their Web site, or the student constitution or bylaws to determine whether your school has a referendum procedure, and to learn what steps you must take to qualify for the ballot.

Push Administrators to Endorse the Emerald Initiative

The Emerald Initiative is SAFER's response to the Amethyst Initiative, which, as we described previously, is a call by several university presidents for a debate about whether to lower the legal drinking age in the United States to eighteen years of age. The Emerald Initiative calls on college presidents and chancellors—particularly those who have signed on to the Amethyst Initiative—to "support an informed and dispassionate public debate" on whether allowing college students to use marijuana more freely could result in fewer students engaging in dangerous drinking. University offi-cials may be reluctant to endorse the Emerald Initiative, so you will need the student body to apply both direct and public pressure. Seek meetings with your student representatives and urge their support. If school leaders do not endorse the initiative, launch a campus cam-paign to highlight that your president or chancellor is ignoring an alternative solution to alcohol-related violence on campus.

Student Government and Elections

In addition to being a leader on campus yourself, you can encourage other existing or potential leaders to further the "marijuana is safer than alcohol" message and to push for corresponding campus policies. You can start by reaching out to members of your student govern-ment—especially any you already know—and gauge their support on the issue. If you find one or more who are supportive, ask them to work with you on a SAFER-specific referendum or resolution, or on a resolution in support of the Emerald Initiative. They might also be able to assist you when it comes to working with administrators. Of course, if you are interested in taking a more hands-on approach to working with the student government, you could run for office your-self and use the SAFER message as part of your campaign platform.

Another way to influence student government is to develop a candidate survey and distribute it to those running for relevant offic-es. Ask whether they agree with the general premises of a SAFER referendum and the Emerald Initiative, and whether they would introduce, support, or oppose such measures. You can use this infor-mation to mobilize members of your organization and to persuade the broader student body to vote for the supportive candidates (or against potential opponents). You will also find out which incoming student leaders are most likely to work with you in the future.

Organize Public Events

As a part of a recognized campus organization, you will have opportunities to host campus forums or panel discussions to debate whether the existing university policies surrounding marijuana and alcohol are making your campus less safe. You could also organize a screening of a relevant film, such as *Death by Alcohol*, the thirty-minute documentary on the alcohol overdose death of Colorado State University student Samantha Spady, or *Grass*, which summarizes the history of marijuana prohibition. Guest speakers also have potential to draw a crowd, so if your group is able to get student activity or event funding, you can reach out to SAFER, NORML, MPP, and other marijuana–policy reform organizations to see whether it would be possible to bring one of their representatives to your school for a speaking engagement.

Generate Media Coverage

We also encourage you or your group to engage in public actions that generate media coverage and draw attention to the "marijuana is safer than alcohol" message. Don't be afraid to be creative, humorous, controversial (within reason), or bizarre (the proverbial "man bites dog" story) in your efforts. For example, you could organize a media conference during the week before a traditionally rowdy football game or other alcohol-fueled event, at which you call on the university to provide a "safer zone" where students have the option of using a less harmful substance than alcohol. Or you could organize a student demonstration in response to a newsworthy alcohol- or marijuana-related incident that occurred on or around campus, such as an assault or alcohol poisoning, or to bring attention to a student being punished harshly for marijuana use.

Getting Active in Your Community—and Online

If you are not a college student, you may be feeling left out at this point. Not to worry—there are also plenty of opportunities to take action in your community or online. Like the campus-specific section, the following ideas for local on-the-ground activism are in no way exhaustive. In fact, we have intentionally omitted certain options, like launching a municipal ballot initiative, that typically entail a level of funding or professional support that is unavailable to most community activists. This is not to say that such activities should be regarded as out of the question. But for now, we are just going to provide you with a few effective and efficient ways to help spread the message

Organize a Safer Community Campaign

As we mentioned in the campus activity section, having an organizational structure upon which to ground your efforts will greatly increase your potential for success. Consider reaching out to any local reform groups that might already exist in the area and gauge their interest on working with you on a "marijuana is safer than alcohol"-style campaign. You could start with NORML, which has more than one hundred chapters located all around the country, and is always interested in helping passionate individuals establish new ones. SAFER does not have local "chapters," but is always ready to provide support and assistance to community leaders.

Distribute Information and Build Organizational Support

You are now an expert when it comes to the relative safety of marijuana compared to alcohol, but far too many of your neighbors are not. Therefore it is up to you to educate them. You can make them aware of the "marijuana is safer than alcohol" message by distributing literature and other educational materials in your community. We recommend attending concerts, festivals, street fairs, and other events that are likely to have a high volume of people. You can also approach potentially supportive local businesses, such as coffee shops and music stores, and ask them if they would be willing to let you leave materials next to their cash registers, in their free publication sections, or on community bulletin boards.

When attending festivals and other popular events, don't forget to bring a clipboard and sign-up sheets so that people interested in getting involved or receiving more information can provide you with their contact information. We also encourage you to consider investing in a SAFER or NORML T-shirt to identify yourself and catch people's attention. Better yet, you could invest in several and use them to raise funds, spread the word, and convey the "marijuana is safer than alcohol" message.

Engage, Educate, and Lobby Elected Officials

Elected representatives need to hear from constituents who support reforming marijuana laws. Chances are that many of them have never been exposed to the message that marijuana is safer than alcohol. So it is up to you to educate them.

Contacting your elected officials is easy, and can be done via e-mail, phone calls, or—ideally—by a personal visit to their local offices. We encourage you to place an emphasis on contacting those officials nearest to you, focusing heavily on your city or town council members and mayor. Once you have been in contact with your locally elected officials, you may also wish to contact your state legislators and governor, as well as your members of Congress.

You can either request a meeting or stop by your local officials' offices. Once you have an opportunity to meet the representative face-to-face, you should inform them of your position and leave them with fact sheets or other information. Be sure to obtain his or her official position on the issue so that you can determine your next steps. For example, you will want to remain in touch with supportive officials, keep them posted on relevant issues (such as major alcohol- or marijuana-related incidents), and seek opportunities to work with them to introduce legislation, raise the debate, and build public and legislative support.

Make the News

You may find this hard to believe, but you have the ability to organize events that will get the "marijuana is safer than alcohol" message out to thousands of citizens. With good timing, an effective hook for the media, and some fun or powerful visuals, television cameras or newspaper photographers will follow. We have seen this occur many times in the past in cities, towns, and campuses across the country. Even if the media doesn't show up, you can capture your event on video and circulate it online. Here are just a few event ideas:

- A press conference in response to news of an alcohol-related incident or increase in crime downtown;
- A call for a moratorium on marijuana citations during traditionally alcohol-fueled events and holidays (for example, St. Patrick's Day); or
- Observing National Alcohol Awareness Month (April) with a visual representation of the relative harms of alcohol and marijuana (for example 300-plus empty beer bottles to represent the number of alcohol overdose deaths in the U.S. each year, next to an empty area to represent those from marijuana)

Whatever public efforts you decide to undertake, just be sure to notify the local newspapers, television networks, and radio stations by sending out a news release or calling them with a heads-up.

Promote the "Marijuana Is Safer Than Alcohol" Message Online

These days, one cannot talk about promoting a cause without discussing online activism and organizing. We are not suggesting that you should build a massive movement of your own; rather, our primary hope is that you will reach out to people within your preexisting networks. As you probably recognize already, there are simply so many opportunities to advance or spread the "marijuana is safer than alcohol" message online. If you have a blog, you can write about the topic whenever it feels appropriate. (You can even write about the fact that you just read this book! Or better yet, you can go to the Web site of Chelsea Green, the publisher of this book, and grab a graphic that you can use to promote the book on your site.)

If you use Twitter, you can send some tweets on the topic—and link to relevant articles or the book itself. On Facebook, you could, for example, set your status to "is thinking about the fact that marijuana is safer than alcohol" (and provide a link to the book) or use the social network to promote local events. We are sure that by the time this book is on the shelves, there will be other new online tools perfect for spreading the "marijuana is safer" message. Be creative and spread the word.

If you are interested in being more aggressive—and helpful—in promoting the "marijuana is safer than alcohol" message, think about responding to articles or blog posts you read online on the subjects of marijuana or alcohol. The simplest way to do this is to post a comment, which is possible on most major news sites and blogs. With all that you have learned in this book, we are certain you will be able to post something thoughtful in response to almost any article about marijuana or alcohol. If you are feeling especially motivated after reading an article on the site of a newspaper or magazine, you could submit a well-crafted letter to the editor, with the hope that it would appear in a print edition and be read by a wide audience. You should be able to find the instructions for submitting a letter to the editor on the publication's Web site, typically in the "opinion" section.

———

If you have read this far, thank you! We hope this extra section has given you plenty of food for thought and we look forward to seeing and hearing about your efforts in the future. Together, by making the fact that marijuana is safer than alcohol conventional wisdom, we will end marijuana prohibition once and for all. Let's get to it!

For more information, visit the following Web sites:

- SAFER: www.SAFERchoice.org or
  www.SAFERcampuses.org
- NORML: www.NORML.org
- MPP: www.MPP.org

Acknowledgments

We would like to express our deepest gratitude to Margo Baldwin, President and Publisher of Chelsea Green, for giving this book the green light. It was a dream long in the making and we thank her for turning it into reality. We would also like to thank the other members of the Chelsea Green team who worked with us throughout the process, including Joni Praded, Peg O'Donnell, Jonathan Teller-Elsberg, Emily Foote, Brianne Goodspeed, Allison Lennox, Taylor Haynes, Makenna Goodman, and, of course, our editor, Cannon Labrie. Thank you to Patricia Stone and to Peter Holm for their work on the cover.

We would also like to thank several experts in the fields of marijuana and marijuana policy who took time to review drafts, offer editorial suggestions, and ensure accuracy. In particular, we would like to thank Franjo Grotenhermen, Gero Leson, Greg Carter, Mitch Earleywine, Allen St. Pierre, and Dale Gieringer.

This book likely never would have been published were it not for the establishment and success of SAFER. Thus, we would like to express our sincere appreciation to the Marijuana Policy Project, the MPP Grants Program, Peter Lewis, Rob Kampia, and the MPP staff for their ongoing support of the organization. We would also like to thank Evan Ackerfeld, who took a leap of faith and followed Mason to Colorado to help get SAFER off the ground; John Foland, SAFER's volunteer webmaster, who has been instrumental in spreading the "marijuana is safer than alcohol" message around the nation and the world; the SAFER and SAFER Voter Education

Fund boards of directors; and SAFER's countless volunteers and supporters, who have donated their time, energy, and money toward advancing the SAFER message.

Individually, the authors would like to acknowledge the following people.

Steve would like to thank his parents, Ron and Joan, for their unconditional support and constant encouragement. He would also like to thank his wife, Lisa, and his two wonderful daughters for their love, their spirit, and their energy, as well as for their patience while he was off spending hundreds of weekend hours writing this book.

Paul would like to thank his wife, Beth, for her unwavering support of this project.

Mason would like to thank his parents, Diane and Steve, for their guidance and encouragement, as well as for their dedication to providing him with an endless array of opportunity. He would also like to thank his sister, Jordan, and his grandparents, David Tvert and Helen and Leo Shuller, who have supported him at every turn. Finally, Mason would like to thank Dr. Rick Mayes for inspiring him to lead with his mind and follow his heart after college, and Steve Fox, who has patiently helped him do so.

Notes

Introduction

1. Paul Kelso, "It's OK to Smoke Dope, England Fans Told," *The Guardian* (UK), June 11, 2004.
2. U.S. Department of Justice, Bureau of Justice Statistics, National Crime Victimization Survey 2002.
3. R. Hingson et al., "Magnitude of Alcohol-Related Mortality and Morbidity among U.S. College Students Ages 18–24: Changes from 1998 to 2001," *Annual Review of Public Health* 26 (2005): 259–79.
4. From the Amethyst Initiative Web site, http://www.amethystinitiative. org/about/ (accessed May 15, 2009).
5. U.S. Office of Applied Studies, *2007 National Survey on Drug Use and Health: Detailed Tables*, http://oas.samhsa.gov/NSDUH/2k7NSDUH/ tabs/Sect1peTabs1to46.htm#Tab1.1A
6. U.S. Department of Justice, Drug Enforcement Administration, *In the Matter of Marijuana Rescheduling Petition (Docket No. 86-22): Opinion and Recommended Ruling, Findings of Fact, Conclusions of Law and Decision of Administrative Law Judge Francis L. Young*, Washington, D.C., September 6, 1988.
7. National Institute on Alcohol Abuse and Alcoholism, *NIAAA Strategic Plan for Research, 2009–2014: Alcohol across the Lifespan*, p. 25; http:// www.niaaa.nih.gov. (accessed January 23, 2009).
8. W. Fals-Stewart, "The Occurrence of Partner Physical Aggression on Days of Alcohol Consumption: A Longitudinal Diary Study, *Journal of Consulting and Clinical Psychology* 71, no. 1 (2003): 41–52.
9. L. Greenfield and M. Henneberg, "Alcohol, Crime, and the Criminal Justice System," Alcohol & Crime: Research and Practice for Prevention, Alcohol Policy XII Conference, Washington, D.C., June 11–14, 2000.
10. Alan Travis, "Blitz on 'Happy Hour' Pubs after 21% Rise in Thuggery," *The Guardian* (UK), April 30, 2004.

Chapter 1

1. Ronald Siegel, *Intoxication: The Universal Drive for Mind-Altering Substances* (Rochester, Vt.: Park Street Press, 2005).

2. Stuart Walton, *Out of It: A Cultural History of Intoxication* (New York: Three Rivers Press, 2003).
3. Andrew Weil and Winifred Rosen, *From Chocolate to Morphine: Everything You Need to Know About Mind-Altering Drugs*, 3rd ed. (Boston: Mariner Books, 1998), 11.
4. Ann Manzardo et al., *Alcoholism: The Facts*, 4th ed. (Oxford: Oxford University Press, 2008), 17.
5. Russo et al., "Phytochemical and Genetic Analyses of Ancient Cannabis from Central Asia, *Journal of Experimental Botany* 59 (2008): 4171–82.
6. Degenhardt et al., "Toward a Global View of Alcohol, Tobacco, Cannabis, and Cocaine Use: Findings from the WHO World Mental Health Surveys," *PLOS Medicine* (2008), online journal.
7. U.S. Office of Applied Studies, *2007 National Survey on Drug Use and Health: Detailed Tables*, http://oas.samhsa.gov/NSDUH/2k7NSDUH/tabs/Sect2peTabs1to42.htm#Tab2.1A (accessed December 29, 2008).
8. Ibid.
9. Ibid., http://oas.samhsa.gov/NSDUH/2k7NSDUH/tabs/Sect1peTabs1to46.htm#Tab1.1A
10. Collected annual reports from Monitoring the Future. Documents online at: http://monitoringthefuture.org.
11. "Alcohol Industry in U.S. Profits from Underage Drinking: Study," *Financial Express*, May 3, 2006.
12. Center on Alcohol Marketing and Youth, *Alcohol Advertising on Television, 2001–2007*, June 23, 2008.
13. Jon Gettman, *Lost Taxes and Other Costs of Marijuana Laws*, DrugScience.org. 2007.
14. "Marijuana Is Top U.S. Cash Crop, Pro-Legalization Analysis Says," *Los Angeles Times*, December 18, 2006.
15. Ibid.
16. See http://adage.com/century/campaigns.html
17. "Hazy Screens: Is Hollywood Pushing Marijuana?" *Christian Science Monitor*, May 16, 2008.
18. "Stoner Flicks Have Slowly Seeped into Modern Culture," *Canwest News Service*, August 11, 2008.
19. "Hashville," *New York Daily News*, January 23, 2002.
20. "Legalizing Marijuana Will Ruin a Great Culture," *Central Florida Future*, July 7, 2008.
21. George Dowdall, *College Drinking: Reframing a Social Problem* (New York: Praeger Publishers, 2009), 107.
22. Paul Armentano, "Legalizing Marijuana Tops Obama Online Poll," TheHill.com, December 15, 2008.

Chapter 2

1. This blog post, along with Senator Harkin's letter, are available online at http://wonkette.com/363265/senator-tom-harkin-marijuana-makes-people-sell-their-children

2. "Have You Tried Marijuana at Least Once?" *Time*/CNN poll, conducted by Harris Interactive on October 23–24, 2002.

3. Paul Armentano, "The Truth about D.A.R.E.," Alternet.org, April 4, 2003.

4. L. Hanus, "Pharmacological and Therapeutic Secrets of Plant and Brain (Endo)Cannabinoids," *Medicinal Research Reviews* 29 (2008): 213–71.

5. U.S. Congressional Research Service. *Hemp as an Agricultural Commodity*, January 2005.

6. Rowan Robinson, *The Great Book of Hemp: The Complete Guide to the Environmental, Commercial, and Medicinal Uses of the World's Most Extraordinary Plant* (Rochester, Vt.: Park Street Press, 1995), 129–33.

7. Dale Gieringer et al., *Medical Marijuana Handbook: Practical Guide to the Therapeutic Uses of Marijuana*, 2nd ed. (Oakland, Cal.: Quick American, 2008), 13.

8. Paul Armentano, "Don't Buy the 'Potent Pot' Hype," HuffingtonPost.com, June 16, 2008.

9. Wayne Hall, *A Comparative Appraisal of the Health and Psychological Consequences of Alcohol, Cannabis, Nicotine, and Opiate Use* (University of New South Wales: National Drug and Alcohol Research Centre, 1995).

10. Dale Gieringer, "Marijuana Water Pipe Vaporization Study," *MAPS Bulletin* (Summer 1996).

11. Selena Roberts, "Marijuana and Pro Basketball: A Special Report," *New York Times*, October 26, 1997.

12. "Seven in Ten Drug Users Are Full-Time Workers," Associated Press, September 8, 1999.

13. Suris et al., "Characteristics of Cannabis Users Who Have Never Smoked Tobacco," *Archives of General Psychiatry* 161 (2007): 1042–47.

14. Robert Kaestner, *The Effect of Illicit Drug Use on Wages of Young Adults*, National Bureau of Economic Research (NBER), Working Paper no. W3535, 1990.

15. Osborne et al., "Understanding the Motivations for Recreational Marijuana Use among Canadians, *Substance Use & Misuse* 43 (2008): 581–83.

Chapter 3

1. Hobbs et al., "Hypnotics and Sedatives; Ethanol," in *The Pharmacological Basis of Therapeutics*, 9th ed., eds. Goodman and Gilman (New York: McGraw Hill, 1996).

2. Ibid.

3. Molly Siple, *Eating for Recovery: The Essential Nutrition Plan to Reverse the Physical Damage of Alcoholism* (Cambridge, Mass.: De Capo Press, 2008).

4. Rob Stein, "A Drink a Day Raises Women's Risk of Cancer, Study Indicates," *Washington Post*, February 25, 2009.

5. Joy Bauer, "Is Wine Good for You?" MSNBC, June 4, 2008.

6. Claire Hughes, "Beer Increases Bone Strength," *Student British Medical Journal* 10 (2002): 441–84.

7. Mukamal et al., "Prior Alcohol Consumption and Mortality Following Acute Myocardial Infarction," *Journal of the American Medical Association* 285 (2001): 1965–70.

8. D. Vinson, "Marijuana and Other Illicit Drug Use and Risk of Injury: A Case-Control Study," *Missouri Medicine* 103 (2006): 152–56.

9. Gmel et al., "Alcohol and Cannabis Use as Risk Factors for Injury—A Case-Crossover Analysis in a Swiss Hospital Emergency Department," *BMC Public Health* (2009), online journal.

10. "One in Six Drivers Drink Sometimes: Report," Reuters News Wire, April 23, 2008.

11. Web site of the U.S. National Institute on Alcohol Abuse and Alcoholism, http://pubs.niaaa.nih.gov/publications/arh25-1/20-31.htm (accessed December 24, 2008).

12. U.S. Department of Justice, Bureau of Justice Statistics, National Crime Victimization Survey 2002.

13. Paul et al., "Association of Alcohol Consumption with Brain Volume in the Framingham Study," *Archives of Neurology* 65 (2008): 1363–67.

14. U.S. Centers for Disease Control, *National Vital Statistics Report*, April 19, 2006.

15. Siple, *Eating for Recovery*, 13.

16. National Institute on Alcohol Abuse and Alcoholism, *NIAAA Strategic Plan for Research, 2009–2014: Alcohol across the Lifespan*, p. 25; http://www.niaaa.nih.gov. (accessed January 23, 2009).

17. Kahn et al., "Stable Behavior Associated with Adults' 10-Year Change in Body Mass Index and Likelihood of Gain at the Waist," *American Journal of Public Health* 87 (1997): 747–54.

18. Manzardo et al., *Alcoholism*, 27.

19. Web site of the U.S. Centers for Disease Control, http://www.cdc.gov/alcohol/faqs.htm (accessed December 24, 2008).

20. Manzardo et al., *Alcoholism*, 30.

21. Dan Childes, "Alcohol Problems Plague 1 out of 3 Americans," ABC News, July 2, 2007.

22. Mokdad et al., "Alcohol Causes of Death in the United States, 2000," *Journal of the American Medical Association* 291 (2004): 1238–45.

23. U.S. Department of Justice, Drug Enforcement Administration, *In the Matter of Marijuana Rescheduling Petition (Docket No. 86-22): Opinion and Recommended Ruling, Findings of Fact, Conclusions of Law and Decision of*

Administrative Law Judge Francis L. Young, Washington, D.C., September 6, 1988.

24. Robert Melamede, "Harm Reduction—The Cannabis Paradox," *Harm Reduction Journal* (2005), online journal.

25. Ethan Russo, "Clinical Endocannabinoid Deficiency: Can This Concept Explain the Therapeutic Benefits of Cannabis in Migraine, Fibromyalgia, and Irritable Bowel Syndrome, and Other Treatment-Resistant Conditions?" *Neuroendocrinology Letters* 25 (2004): 31–39.

26. Sidney et al., "Marijuana Use and Mortality," *American Journal of Public Health* 87 (1997): 585–90.

27. Sidney et al., "Marijuana Use and Cancer Incidence," *Cancer, Causes & Controls* 8 (1997): 722–28.

28. Adreasson et al., "Cannabis Use and Mortality among Young Men," *Scandinavian Journal of Public Health* 18 (1990): 9–15.

29. Vinson, "Marijuana and Other Illicit Drug Use and Risk of Injury."

30. Gmel, "Alcohol and Cannabis Use as Risk Factors for Injury."

31. Goldschmidt et al., "Prenatal Marijuana Exposure and Intelligence Test Performance at Age 6," *Journal of the American Academy of Child and Adolescent Psychiatry* 47 (2008): 254–63.

32. U.S. National Academy of Sciences, Institute of Medicine, *Marijuana and Medicine: Assessing the Science Base* (Washington, D.C., 1999).

33. Ibid.

34. Abrams et al., "Cannabis in Painful HIV-associated Sensory Neuropathy," *Neurology* 68 (2007): 515–21.

35. Hampson et al., "Cannabidiol and Delta9-tetrahydrocannabinol Are Neuroprotective Antioxidants," *Proceedings of the National Academy of Sciences of the USA* 95 (1998): 8268–73.

36. See http://www.patentstorm.us/patents/6630507.html

37. Rog et al., "Oromucosal Delta-9-tetrahydrocannabinol/cannabidiol for Neuropathic Pain Associated with Multiple Sclerosis: An Uncontrolled, Open-label, 2-year Extension Trial," *Clinical Therapeutics* 29 (2007): 2068–79. See also: Wade et al., "Long-term Use of a Cannabis-based Medicine in the Treatment of Spasticity and Other Symptoms of Multiple Sclerosis," *Multiple Sclerosis* 12 (2006): 639–45.

38. Pryce et al., "Cannabinoids Inhibit Neurodegeneration in Models of Multiple Sclerosis," *Brain* 126 (2003): 2191–2202.

39. Raman et al., "Amyotrophic Lateral Sclerosis: Delayed Disease Progression in Mice by Treatment with a Cannabinoid," *Amyotrophic Lateral Sclerosis & Other Motor Neuron Disorders* 5 (2004): 33–39.

40. Joel Rozen, "A Higher Calling," *Creative Loafing Sarasota,* January 8, 2008.

41. Lu et al., "The Cannabinergic System as a Target for Anti-inflammatory Diseases," *Journal of Neuroimmunology* 166 (2006): 3–18.

42. Appendino et al., "Antibacterial Cannabinoids from *Cannabis sativa*: A Structure-activity Study," *Journal of Natural Products* 71 (2008): 1427–30.

43. Sarfaraz et al, "Cannabinoids for Cancer Treatment: Progress and Promise," *Cancer Research* 68 (2008): 339–42.

44. Manuel Guzman, "Cannabinoids: Potential Anticancer Agents," *Nature Reviews Cancer* 3 (2003): 745–55.

45. Raymond Cushing, "Pot Shrinks Tumors: Government Knew in '74," Alternet.org, May 31, 2000.

46. Ashtari et al., "Diffusion Abnormalities in Adolescents and Young Adults with a History of Heavy Cannabis Use," *Journal of Psychiatric Research* 43 (2009): 189–204.

47. Whan et al., "Effects of Delta-9-tetrahydrocannabinol, the Primary Psychoactive Cannabinoid in Marijuana, on Human Sperm Function in Vitro," *Fertility and Sterility* 85 (2006): 653–60.

48. Tashkin et al., "Effects of Marijuana on Experimentally Induced Asthma," *American Review of Respiratory Disease* 112 (1975): 377–86.

49. William J. Cromie, "Marijuana Said to Trigger Heart Attacks," *Harvard University Gazette*, March 2, 2000.

50. Parfieniuk et al., "Role of Cannabinoids in Liver Disease," *World Journal of Gastroenterology* 14 (2008): 6109–14.

51. Sylvestre et al., "Cannabis Use Improves Retention and Virological Outcomes in Patients Treated with Hepatitis C," *European Journal of Gastroenterology & Hepatology* 18 (2006): 1057–63.

52. Moore et al., "Cannabis Use and Risk of Psychotic or Affective Mental Health Outcomes: A Systemic Review," *Lancet* 370 (2007): 319–28.

53. Ferdinand et al., "Cannabis Use Predicts Future Psychotic Symptoms, and Vice Versa" *Addiction* 100 (2005): 612–18.

54. Ashton et al., "Cannabinoids in Bipolar Affective Disorder: A Review and Discussion of Their Therapeutic Potential," *Journal of Psychopharmacology* 19 (2005): 187–94.

55. Wayne Hall, *A Comparative Appraisal of the Health and Psychological Consequences of Alcohol, Cannabis, Nicotine, and Opiate Use* (University of New South Wales: National Drug and Alcohol Research Centre, 1995).

56. David Concar, "High Anxieties: What the WHO Doesn't Want You to Know about Cannabis," *New Scientist*, February 21, 2008.

57. Reuters News Wire, "French Report Says Drinking Worse Than Cannabis," June 16, 1998.

58. Meyers et al., *Twentieth Annual Report of the Research Advisory Panel, 1989: Prepared for the Governor and Legislature* (Sacramento, Cal., 1989).

59. Special Senate Committee on Illegal Drugs. *Final Report: Cannabis: Our Position for a Canadian Public Policy* (Ottawa, 2002).

60. Australian Institute of Health and Welfare, *The Burden of Disease and Injury in Australia, 2003* (Canberra, 2007).

61. Nutt et al., "Development of a Rational Scale to Assess the Harms of Drugs of Potential Misuse," *Lancet* 369 (2007): 1047–53.

62. The Beckley Foundation, *Global Cannabis Commission Report—Cannabis Policy: Moving Beyond Stalemate* (Oxford, 2008).

Chapter 4

1. Lester Grinspoon, *Marihuana Reconsidered*, 2nd ed. (Oakland, Cal.: Quick American Archives, 1994).
2. United States Department of Agriculture, *Yearbook of the United States Department of Agriculture* (Washington, D.C.: USDA, 1913).
3. Dale Gieringer, *The Origins of Cannabis Prohibition in California*, rev. ed. (San Francisco: NORML, 2006), http://www.canorml.org/background/caloriginsmjproh.pdf
4. Ibid.
5. David Musto, "History of the Marihuana Tax Act," *Archives of General Psychiatry* 26 (1972): 101–8.
6. Ron Mann, *Grass: The Paged Experience* (Toronto: Warwick Publishing, 2001).
7. Ibid.
8. Gieringer, *The Origins of Cannabis Prohibition in California*, 35.
9. Richard Bonnie and Charles Whitebread, *The Marijuana Conviction: A History of Marijuana Prohibition in the United States* (New York: The Lindesmith Center, 1999).
10. As cited in Larry Sloman, *Reefer Madness: A History of Marijuana*, 2nd ed. (New York: St. Martin's/Griffin, 1998).
11. Grinspoon, *Marihuana Reconsidered*, 17.
12. *Grass: The Movie*, directed by Ronn Mann, 2000.
13. Sloman, *Reefer Madness: A History of Marijuana*, 60.
14. Bonnie and Whitebread, *The Marijuana Conviction*, 100–101.
15. As cited by Rowan Robinson, *The Great Book of Hemp: The Complete Guide to the Environmental, Commercial, and Medicinal Uses of the World's Most Extraordinary Plant* (Rochester, Vt.: Park Street Press, 1995), 147.
16. Sloman, *Reefer Madness: A History of Marijuana*, 66.
17. Ibid., 68.
18. Bonnie and Whitebread, *The Marijuana Conviction*, 165–66.
19. Sloman, *Reefer Madness: A History of Marijuana*, 76.
20. Bonnie and Whitebread, *The Marijuana Conviction*, 172.
21. Ibid., 172–73.
22. Sloman, *Reefer Madness: A History of Marijuana*, 80.
23. Bonnie and Whitebread, *The Marijuana Conviction*, 174.
24. Jon Gettman, *Crimes of Indiscretion: Marijuana Arrests in the United States* (Washington, D.C.: NORML Foundation, 2005), http://www.norml.org/pdf_files/NORML_Crimes_of_Indiscretion.pdf
25. National Commission on Marihuana and Drug Use, *Marihuana: A Signal of Misunderstanding—The Official Report of the National Commission on Marihuana and Drug Abuse* (Washington, D.C., 1972).

26. *Grass: The Movie.*
27. Ibid.
28. Gettman, *Crimes of Indiscretion*, 51.

Chapter 5

1. Reuters News Wire, "U.S. Marijuana Even Stronger Than Before: Report," April 25, 2007.
2. Associated Press, "Locals Ask State Help to Battle Pot Houses," June 22, 2007.
3. ElSohly et al., "Potency Trends of Delta9-THC and Other Cannabinoids in Confiscated Marijuana from 1980–1997," *Journal of Forensic Sciences* 45 (2000): 24–30.
4. Lynn Zimmer and John P. Morgan, *Marijuana Myths, Marijuana Facts: A Review of the Scientific Evidence* (New York: Lindesmith Center, 1997), 137.
5. Craig Reinarman, "Cannabis Policies and User Practices: Market Separation, Price, Potency, and Accessibility in Amsterdam and San Francisco," *International Journal of Drug Policy* 20 (2009): 28–37.
6. Heishman et al., "Effects of Tetrahydrocannabinol Content on Marijuana Smoking Behavior, Subjective Reports, and Performance," *Pharmacology, Biochemistry, and Behavior* 34 (1989): 173–79.
7. Abrams et al., "Vaporization as a Smokeless Cannabis Delivery System: A Pilot Study," *Clinical Pharmacology and Therapeutics* 82 (2007): 572–78.
8. Karen Tandy, "Marijuana: The Myths Are Killing Us," *Police Chief Magazine* (March 2005).
9. U.S. Office of Applied Studies, *2007 National Survey on Drug Use and Health: Detailed Tables*, http://oas.samhsa.gov/NSDUH/2k7NSDUH/tabs/Sect1peTabs1to46.htm#Tab1.1A (accessed December 29, 2008).
10. Ibid.
11. Netherlands Institute of Mental Health and Addiction, *Cannabis Policy: An Update*. (Utrecht: Trimbos Institute, 1997).
12. Ask the White House, Q&A with John Walters, January 7, 2005; archived at http://blogs.salon.com/0002762/stories/2007/10/09/theDrugCzar IsRequiredByLaw.html
13. Nutt et al., "Development of a Rational Scale to Assess the Harms of Drugs of Potential Misuse," *Lancet* 369 (2007): 1047–53; Phillip Hilts, "Is Nicotine Addictive? It Depends Whose Criteria You Use," *New York Times*, August 2, 1994.
14. U.S. National Academy of Sciences, Institute of Medicine, *Marijuana and Medicine: Assessing the Science Base* (Washington, D.C., 1999).
15. Ibid.
16. Jan Copeland and Jane Maxwell, "Cannabis Treatment Outcomes among Legally Coerced and Non-coerced Adults," *BMC Public Health* 7 (2007), open access journal.

17. U.S. Department of Health and Human Services: Substance Abuse Mental Health Services Administration, *2006 Treatment Episode Data Set (TEDS)—Highlights*, http://www.oas.samhsa.gov/teds2k6highlights/Tbl3.htm (accessed March 5, 2009).

18. U.S. Drug Enforcement Administration, DEA Briefs and Background: Marijuana, http://www.usdoj.gov/dea/concern/marijuana.html (accessed March 5, 2009).

19. Abrams et al., "Vaporization As a Smokeless Cannabis Delivery System."

20. Sidney et al., "Marijuana Use and Cancer Incidence," *Cancer, Causes and Control* 8 (1997): 722–28.

21. Hashibe et al., "Marijuana Use and the Risk of Lung Cancer and Upper Aerodigestive Tract Cancer: Results of a Population-based Case-control Study," *Cancer Epidemiology Biomarkers & Prevention* 15 (2006): 1829–34.

22. Marc Kaufman, "Study Finds No Cancer-Marijuana Connection," *Washington Post*, May 26, 2006.

23. Tandy, "Marijuana: The Myths Are Killing Us."

24. Menetrey et al., "Assessment of Driving Capability through the Use of Clinical and Psychomotor Tests in Relation to Blood Cannabinoid Levels Following Oral Administration of 20mg Dronabinol or of a Cannabis Decoction Made with 20 and 60mg delta-9-THC," *Journal of Analytical Toxicology* 29 (2005): 327–38.

25. Ronen et al., "Effects of THC on Driving Performance, Physiological State and Subjective Feelings Relative to Alcohol," *Accident: Analysis and Prevention* 40 (2008): 926–34.

26. Alison Smiley, "Marijuana: On-Road and Driving-Simulator Studies," in *The Health Effects of Cannabis*, eds. Kalant et al, (Toronto: Canadian Centre for Addiction and Mental Health, 1999): 173–91.

27. Paul Armentano, *Cannabis and Driving: A Scientific and Rational Review* (Washington, D.C.: NORML Foundation, 2008), http://norml.org/pdf_files/NORML_Cannabis_And_Driving.pdf

28. Bedard et al., "The Impact of Cannabis on Driving," *Canadian Journal of Public Health* 98 (2007): 6–11.

29. Laumon et al., "Cannabis Intoxication and Fatal Road Crashes in France: A Population based Case-control Study," *British Medical Journal* 331 (2005): 1371–77.

30. http://www.syndistar.com/product_media/pdfs/pbda113.pdf

31. Miranda Marquit, "Is Marijuana Less Dangerous Than Alcohol?" PhysOrg.com, March 26, 2009.

32. Squeglia et al., "The Influence of Substance Use on Adolescent Brain Development," *Clinical EEG and Neuroscience* 40 (2009): 31–38.

33. Tzilos et al., "Lack of Hippocampal Volume Change in Long-term Heavy Cannabis Users," *American Journal on Addictions* 14 (2005): 64–72.

34. Lyons et al., "Neuropsychological Consequences of Regular Marijuana Use: A Twin Study," *Psychological Medicine* 34 (2004): 1239–50.

35. Fried et al., "Current and Former Marijuana Use: Preliminary Findings of a Longitudinal Study of Effects on IQ in Young Adults," *CMAJ* 166 (2002): 887–91.
36. Pope et al., "Neuropsychological Performance in Long-term Cannabis Users, *Archives in General Psychiatry* 58 (2001): 909–15.
37. Paul Armentano, *Cannabis and the Brain: A User's Guide* (Washington, D.C.: NORML Foundation. 2006), http://norml.org/pdf_files/NORML_Cannabis_And_The_Brain.pdf
38. Jiang et al., "Cannabinoids Promote Embryonic and Adult Hippocampus Neurogenesis and Produce Anxiolytic- and Depressant-like Effects," *The Journal of Clinical Investigation* 115 (2005): 3104–16; Dawn Walton, "Study Turns Pot Wisdom on Head," *Globe and Mail*, October 14, 2005.
39. National Commission on Marihuana and Drug Abuse, *Marihuana: A Signal of Misunderstanding—The Official Report of the National Commission on Marihuana and Drug Abuse* (Washington, D.C., 1972).
40. Special Senate Committee on Illegal Drugs, *Final Report: Cannabis: Our Position for a Canadian Public Policy* (Ottawa, 2002).
41. Advisory Council on the Misuse of Drugs, *The Classification of Cannabis under the Misuse of Drugs Act of 1971* (London, 2002).
42. Blondell et al., "Toxicology Screening Results: Injury Associations Among Hospitalized Trauma Patients," *The Journal of Trauma* 58 (2005): 561–70.
43. National Drug Intelligence Center, *National Drug Threat Assessment, 2004*, (Johnstown, Penn., 2004).
44. Philip Johnston, "Cannabis Use 'Will Impair But Not Damage Mental Health,'" *The Telegraph*, January 23, 2006.
45. Leslie Iverson, "Long-term Effects of Exposure to Cannabis," *Current Opinions in Pharmacology* 5 (2005): 69–72.

Chapter 6

1. Andy Borowitz, "Phelps Congratulates Cardinals on Super Bowl Win," HuffingtonPost.com, February 2, 2009.
2. CNN.com, "Phelps Suspended from Competition, Dropped by Kellogg," February 6, 2009, http://www.cnn.com/2009/US/02/05/kellogg. phelps/index.html
3. Paul Armentano, "20 Million Arrests and Counting," *In These Times*, October 2008.
4. Paul Armentano, "How Can We Discuss Marijuana Policy When America's Top Cop Won't Even Acknowledge the Facts?" TheHill.com, September 23, 2008.
5. See http://blog.mpp.org/?p=173
6. Bill McClellan, "Phelps Story Shows Why We Should Say No to Drug War," *St. Louis Post-Dispatch*, February 9, 2009.
7. See http://ssdp.org/campaigns/srp/legislative.php

8. Sam Amick, "Kings' Miller Vows He'll Rebound after Suspension, *Sacramento Bee*, July 18, 2008.

9. Daniel Forbes, "Fighting 'Cheech and Chong' Medicine," Salon.com, July 31, 2000.

10. Ibid.

11. Ibid.

12. Mark Eddy, "War on Drugs: The National Youth Anti-Drug Media Campaign," CRS Report for Congress, Congressional Research Service, April 10, 2003.

13. Daniel Forbes, "Prime-Time Propaganda," Salon.com, January 13, 2000.

14. Ibid.

15. Daniel Forbes, "The Quiet Death of Prime-Time Propaganda," Salon.com, June 30, 2001.

16. Ibid.

17. Jayme Blaschke, "Anti-drug Ads Can Boomerang, Study Discovers," Texas State University News Service, May 28, 2004.

18. "Federal Budget: Drug Czar's Ad Campaign Takes a Hit, DC Can Do Needle Exchange, But More Funding for Law Enforcement," *Drug War Chronicle*, December 21, 2007.

19. NORML news advisory, "National Association of Broadcasters Enlisted in War on Marijuana," June 19, 1997.

20. "Magazine Publishers of America Enlist in Drug War Media Blitz," October 22, 1998.

21. "Office of National Drug Control Policy—Video News Release," U.S. Government Accountability Office, January 4, 2005.

22. Ibid.

23. All figures in this paragraph courtesy Open Secrets, http://www.open secrets.org

24. See http://www.cspinet.org/booze/underagedrinking.ondcp2.htm

25. As of May 2009, this language appeared in the Unites States Code at 21 U.S.C. 1708(j)(2).

26. Scott Morgan, "Why Do Prison and Alcohol Lobbies Oppose Drug Treatment?" StoptheDrugWar.org, October 22, 2008.

Chapter 7

1. Marc Fisher, "On Campus, Legal Drinking Age Is Flunking the Reality Test," *Washington Post*, August 21, 2008.

2. George W. Dowdall, *College Drinking: Reframing a Social Problem* (Westport, Conn.: Praeger Publishers, 2009), 152.

3. Laura Hoffman, "Referendum Hopes to Reform Marijuana Policy," *The Exponent* (Purdue's "Independent Daily Student Newspaper"), February 25, 2009.

4. Carrie Wells, "Activist's Past Bars Her from University Senate," *University of Maryland Diamondback*, March 10, 2008.

5. Dowdall, *College Drinking*, 27.
6. Ibid.
7. Ibid., 49.
8. R. Hingson et al., "Magnitude of Alcohol-Related Mortality and Morbidity among U.S. College Students Ages 18-24: Changes from 1998 to 2001," *Annual Review of Public Health*, 26 (2005): 259–79.
9. Ibid.
10. Ibid.
11. National Center on Addiction and Substance Abuse at Columbia University, *Rethinking Rites of Passage: Substance Abuse on America's Campuses* (New York: 1994), ii.
12. http://www.e-chug.com/
13. H. Harwood et al., *The Economic Costs of Alcohol and Drug Abuse in the United States 1992*, Report prepared for the National Institute on Drug Abuse and the National Institute on Alcohol Abuse and Alcoholism, National Institutes of Health, Department of Health and Human Services. NIH publication no. 98-4327 (Rockville, Md.: National Institutes of Health, 1998), section 5.3.7.
14. H. Harwood, *Updating Estimates of the Economic Costs of Alcohol Abuse in the United States: Estimates, Update Methods, and Data*, report prepared by The Lewin Group for the National Institute on Alcohol Abuse and Alcoholism, 2000; based on estimates, analyses, and data reported in Harwood et al., *The Economic Costs of Alcohol and Drug Abuse in the United States 1992*.
15. T. Babor, *Alcohol: No Ordinary Commodity* (New York: Oxford University Press, 2003).
16. David T. Levy et al., "Costs of Underage Drinking," Pacific Institute for Research & Evaluation, the Underage Drinking Enforcement Training Center, U.S. Department of Justice, Office of Justice Programs, Office of Juvenile Justice and Delinquency Prevention (OJJDP), updated edition, June 1999.
17. G. B. Thomas and C. G. Davis, "Comparing the Perceived Seriousness and Actual Costs of Substance Abuse in Canada: Analysis Drawn from the 2004 Canadian Additional Survey" (Ottawa: Canadian Centre on Substance Abuse, 2006).
18. Office of National Drug Control Policy, *The Economic Costs of Drug Abuse in the United States, 1992-1998*, publication no. NCJ-190636 (Washington, D.C.: Executive Office of the President, 2001).
19. Scott Boeck, "Coors Field Faces Suit over 'Safe Attendance,'" *USA Today*, September 27, 2005.
20. Mark Maske, "NFL Spectators Being Watched More Closely," *Washington Post*, September 7, 2008.
21. See http://www.cspinet.org/booze/ondcp.htm

22. Harwood et al., *The Economic Costs of Alcohol and Drug Abuse in the United States 1992*, section 6.2.3.1.
23. Ibid.
24. National Institute on Alcohol Abuse and Alcoholism, *NIAAA Strategic Plan for Research, 2009-2014: Alcohol across the Lifespan*, http://www.niaaa.nih.gov. (accessed January 23, 2009).
25. U.S. Department of Justice, Bureau of Justice Statistics, National Crime Victimization Survey 2002.
26. WHO Policy Briefing, "Alcohol and Violence: Interpersonal Violence and Alcohol," World Health Organization (2006).
27. W. Fals-Stewart, "The Occurrence of Partner Physical Aggression on Days of Alcohol Consumption: A Longitudinal Diary Study," *Journal of Consulting and Clinical Psychology* 71, no. 1 (2003): 41–52.
28. W. Fals-Stewart, "Intimate Partner Violence and Substance Use: A Longitudinal Day-to-Day Examination," *Addictive Behaviors* 28 (2003): 1555–74.
29. This appearance by Chris Carter can be found at: http://espnradio.espn.go.com/espnradio/clipArchive?showID=mikeandmike

Chapter 8

1. For further details regarding the Commission and its recommendations, please see chapter 4.
2. Chris Bowers, "Legalizing Marijuana More Popular Than Republicans," OpenLeft.com, February 20, 2009.
3. Jon Gettman, "Lost Taxes and Other Costs of Marijuana Laws," DrugScience.org, 2007.
4. Press statement of Betty Yee, chairwoman, California Board of Equalization, February 23, 2009.
5. Dale Gieringer, *Legalization Could Yield California Taxpayers Over $1.2 Billion Per Year: Additional Spinoff Benefits Up To $12–$18 Billion*, California NORML, February 2009, http://www.canorml.org/background/CA_legalization2.html
6. Federal Bureau of Investigation, *Crime in America: FBI Uniform Crime Reports 2007* (Washington, D.C., 2008).
7. Jeffrey Miron, *Budgetary Implications of Marijuana Prohibition in the United States* (Washington, D.C.: Marijuana Policy Project, 2005), http://www.prohibitioncosts.org/mironreport.html
8. Gettman, "Lost Taxes and Other Costs of Marijuana Laws."
9. U.S. Bureau of Justice Statistics, *Drug Use and Dependence, State and Federal Prisoners, 2004* (Washington, D.C., 2006).
10. Paul Armentano, "A Billion Dollars a Year for Pot?" *Washington Examiner*, October 18, 2006.

11. A 2003 evaluation of the Washington, D.C., police department determined that it took a police officer, on average, 7.7 hours to complete the required paperwork associated with a criminal arrest.

12. NORML news advisory, "Drug War Priorities Shift from Hard Drugs to Marijuana, Arrest Figures Reveal," July 8, 1999.

13. New York Civil Liberties Union, *The Marijuana Arrest Crusade in New York City: Racial Bias in Police Policy 1997–2007* (New York, 2008).

14. Benson et al., "The Impact of Drug Enforcement on Crime: An Investigation of the Opportunity Cost of Police Resources," *Journal of Drug Issues* 31 (2001): 989–1006.

15. Jon Gettman, *United States Marijuana Arrests, Part Two: Racial Differences in Drug Arrests* (Washington, D.C.: NORML Foundation, 2000), http://norml.org/index.cfm?Group_ID=5326

16. Jon Gettman, *Crimes of Indiscretion: Marijuana Arrests in the United States* (Washington, D.C.: NORML Foundation, 2005), http://www.norml.org/pdf_files/NORML_Crimes_of_Indiscretion.pdf

17. New York Civil Liberties Union, *The Marijuana Arrest Crusade in New York City.*

18. Gettman, *Crimes of Indiscretion.*

19. U.S. Department of Health and Human Services, Substance Abuse Mental Health Services Association, *Initiation of Marijuana Use: Trends, Patterns, and Implications,* (Washington, D.C., 2008).

20. Janet Kornblum, "Prescription Drugs More Accessible to Teens Than Beer," *USA Today,* August 14, 2008.

21. Robert MacCoun and Peter Reuter, "Evaluating Alternative Cannabis Regimes," *British Journal of Psychiatry* 178 (2001): 123–28.

22. Terry-McElrath et al., "Saying No to Marijuana: Why American Youth Report Quitting and Abstaining," *Journal of Studies on Alcohol and Drugs* 69 (2008): 769–805.

23. Degenhardt et al., "Toward a Global View of Alcohol, Tobacco, Cannabis, and Cocaine Use: Findings from the WHO World Mental Health Surveys," *PLOS Medicine* (2008), online journal.

24. Ibid.

25. Mark Stevenson, "Marijuana Big Earner for Mexico Gangs," Associated Press, February 22, 2008.

Chapter 9

1. Ed Vogel, "Drug Czar Asked For Explanation," *Las Vegas Review Journal,* January 16, 2003.

2. Search "CRCM" at http://sos.state.nv.us/SOSCandidateServices/AnonymousAccess/ReportSearch/ReportSearch.aspx

Chapter 10

1. http://www.youtube.com/watch?v=Wm9jdbF0rEY
2. Alan Gathright, "Pro-Pot Group Aims at State Law in '06," *Rocky Mountain News*, December 28, 2005.
3. The Office of National Drug Control Policy, "Pete's Couch" ad transcript:

> *(Scene opens with a guy sitting on the couch talking directly to the camera)*
> "I smoked weed and nobody died. I didn't get into a car accident, I didn't O.D. on heroin the next day, nothing happened."
> *(Shot widens to show the guy with two friends sitting on the couch)*
> "We sat on Pete's couch for eleven hours. Now what's going to happen on Pete's couch? Nothing."
> *(Shot now shows the guys on the couch in the middle of the woods with some mountain bikers riding by. Then to a basketball court. Then an ice rink.)*
> "You have a better shot of dying out there in the real world, driving hard to the rim, ice skating with a girl. No, you wanna keep yourself alive, go over to Pete's and sit on his couch 'til you're eighty-six. Safest thing in the world."
> *(Shot now shows the guys on the couch outside a movie theater. The guy talking gets up from the couch and walks into the theater)*
> "Me? I'll take my chances out there. Call me reckless."
> See the ad (unless the government takes it down) at: http://www.youtube.com/watch?v=2yfEvfJ9XAw

4. Robert Weller, "Colo. Pro-Pot Ads Target Bush, Cheney," Associated Press, November 5, 2006.
5. "Heed Voters on Pot," *Rocky Mountain News* editorial, May 30, 2008.
6. Douglas Brown, "Grass Roots: 58,866 Denver Residents Voted to Legalize Pot—Among Them, These Moms," *Denver Post*, December 27, 2005.

Chapter 11

1. Malcolm Gladwell, *The Tipping Point: How Little Things Can Make a Big Difference* (New York: Little Brown, 2000), 12.

Chapter 12

1. Rielle Capler and Philippe Lucas, *Guidelines for the Community-Based Distribution of Medical Cannabis in Canada* (Vancouver, B.C.: Vancouver Island Compassion Society: 2006); also found at http://www.the compassionclub.org/resources/guidelines%20for%20distribution.pdf

2. Marijuana Policy Project, *Marijuana Use by Young People: The Impact of State Medical Marijuana Laws* (Washington, D.C., 2008), http://www.mpp.org/assets/pdfs/general/TeenUseReport_0608.pdf

3. U.S. General Accounting Office. *Marijuana: Early Experiences With Four States' Laws That Allow Use For Medical Purposes.* Washington, D.C.: 2002.

4. U.S. Government Accountability Office, *ONDCP Media Campaign: Contractor's National Evaluation Did Not Find that the Youth Anti-Drug Media Campaign Was Effective in Reducing Youth Drug Use: Report to the Subcommittee on Transportation, Treasury, the Judiciary, Housing and Urban Development, and Related Agencies, Committee on Appropriations, U.S. Senate* (Washington, D.C., 2006).

5. CASA Press Release, "National Survey of American Attitudes on Substance Abuse XIII: Teens and Parents," August 14, 2008.

6. Terry-McElrath et al., "Saying No to Marijuana: Why American Youth Report Quitting and Abstaining," *Journal of Studies on Alcohol and Drugs* 69 (2008): 769–805.

7. Reuters News Wire, "U.S. Smoking Rate Is under 20 percent for the First Time," November 13, 2008.

8. Johnson et al., *Marijuana Decriminalization: The Impact on Youth 1975–1980* (Ann Arbor, Mich.: Institute for Social Research, 1981).

9. Marsha Rosenbaum, *Safety First: A Reality-Based Approach to Teens and Drugs,* (San Francisco: Drug Policy Alliance, 2007).

Index

About the Authors

Steve Fox is the Director of State Campaigns for the Marijuana Policy Project (MPP), the nation's largest organization dedicated to reforming marijuana laws. From 2002–2005, he lobbied Congress as MPP's Director of Government Relations. He cofounded Safer Alternative for Enjoyable Recreation (SAFER) in 2005 and has helped guide its operations since its inception. He is a graduate of Tufts University and Boston College Law School and currently lives in Maryland with his wife and two daughters.

Paul Armentano is the deputy director of NORML (The National Organization for the Reform of Marijuana Laws) and the NORML Foundation. A recognized national expert in marijuana policy, health, and pharmacology, he has spoken at dozens of national conferences and legal seminars and has testified before state legislatures and federal agencies. His writing has appeared in over 500 publications. Armentano is the 2008 recipient of the Project Censored Real News Award for Outstanding Investigative Journalism. He currently lives in California with his wife and son.

Mason Tvert is the cofounder and executive director of Safer Alternative for Enjoyable Recreation (SAFER) and the SAFER Voter Education Fund. He appears frequently in the news and travels the country promoting the "Marijuana Is Safer Than Alcohol" message. He resides in Denver, where he serves on the city's Marijuana Policy Review Panel appointed by Mayor John W. Hickenlooper.

Norm Stamper began his law enforcement career in San Diego in 1966 as a beat cop. In 1994 he was named Chief of the Seattle Police Department. Now retired from police work, he is author of *Breaking Rank*.

Ask your doctor which of these is **least** harmful to your health.

Now ask your elected offical why it's **illegal.**

We voted for change. Let's make sure we get it.
Find out how you can help.

888.67.NORML
www.**norml**.org

Marijuana prohibition has failed.
It's time for a new approach.

The **Marijuana Policy Project** is leading the way, making real progress In reforming U.S. marijuana laws, by:

... passing legislation and ballot initiatives to allow seriously ill patients to use medical marijuana with their doctors' recommendations

... working to replace marijuana prohibition with a sensible system of regulation

... lobbying Congress to end the drug czar's deceptive ad campaigns

... and much more.

Change is happening.
Will you join us?

**Marijuana
Policy Project**
www.mpp.org

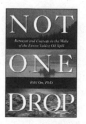

the politics and practice of sustainable living

CHELSEA GREEN PUBLISHING

**HOW THE RICH ARE
DESTROYING THE EARTH**
HERVÉ KEMPF
Foreword by GREG PALAST
ISBN 9781603580359
Paperback • $12.95

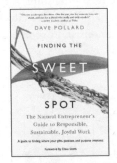

FINDING THE SWEET SPOT
*The Natural Entrepreneur's Guide to
Responsible, Sustainable, Joyful Work*
DAVE POLLARD
Foreword by DAVE SMITH
ISBN 9781933392905
Paperback • $17.95

CLIMATE SOLUTIONS
*A Citizen's Guide: What Works,
What Doesn't, and Why*
PETER BARNES
Foreword by BILL MCKIBBEN
ISBN 9781603580052
Paperback • $9.95

THE PEOPLE V. BUSH
*One Lawyer's Campaign To Bring
the President to Justice and the
National Grassroots Movement
She Encountered Along the Way*
CHARLOTTE DENNETT
ISBN 9781603582094
Paperback • $14.95

For more information or to request a catalog,
visit **www.chelseagreen.com** or
call toll-free **(800) 639-4099**.